ACKNOWLEDGEMENTS

With highest gratitude I dedicate this book most emphatically to God, Jesus Christ, my gorgeous mother Gina M. DiStefano, the greatest woman on earth , father, William M. Staib, grandfather, all-American patriotic hero, Frank M. DiStefano, sweet beloved grandmother, Camille DiStefano, Uncle Michael/Lorraine DiStefano, Aunt Kim/Uncle Dean Carbonaro, their children, Gina/Amanda Carbonaro, Aunt Lucille/Uncle Ric Mango, Christopher/Priscilla Mango, History professor/mentor, Dr. Marilyn Weigold, who personally inspired this work, all other professors over the years, including, inter alia, Dr. Northey, Dr. Roy Girasa, Esq. Prof. George Pappas, Esq., Dr. Margaret Fitzgerald, Esq., Dr. Reza Afshari, Dr. Richard Kraus, Esq., Dr. Peter Edelstein, Esq., Prof. Francis Carroll, every closest friend out there, other special individuals forgotten, or not herein mentioned, who know me personally/professionally, you belong here no less than anyone else aforementioned, iUniverse Publishing, for all their considerable contributions, Nancy Reagan, her family, & of course, our great beloved 40th President Ronald W. Reagan.

Legacy of a Leader

Paradigm of America

Michael W. Staib

iUniverse, Inc.
Bloomington

Legacy of a Leader
Paradigm of America

iUniverse books may be ordered through booksellers or by contacting:

iUniverse
1663 Liberty Drive
Bloomington, IN 47403
www.iuniverse.com
1-800-Authors (1-800-288-4677)

ISBN: 978-1-4620-0590-1 (sc)
ISBN: 978-1-4620-0802-5 (ebook)

Printed in the United States of America

iUniverse rev. date: 06/14/2011

Introduction:

Ronald Wilson Reagan, as 40th President of the United States, entered office on January 20, 1981, concluding a period characterized by political instability and social upheaval. Upon inauguration, at 70 years of age, Reagan became the oldest person, and only professional actor to ever serve as President. His celebrity status alone transformed American perception of subsequent presidents. Hence, "The Great Communicator", became a name associated with his effective exploitation of language and television to present administrative platforms. Reagan's inauguration, following an overwhelming landslide victory, signifies the reassertion of Republican power in Congress, and overall shift toward conservative values among mainstream Americans.

This ideological transition most unequivocally reflects the failed administration of his liberal predecessor Jimmy Carter. Until this time, many people shunned voting Republican due to the residual blemish of Watergate. Nonetheless, Reagan's popularity prevailed. Unlike other presidential incumbents, Reagan stayed true to his party and the conservative principles he championed. Already an American icon by reputation, he eventually progressed to become perhaps the most influential government leader in all of 20th century world history. Few presidents faced adversity with more resolution than Reagan. By conquering communism and its virulent dissemination, his bold initiative alone stands as testament to his profound historical influence.

Reagan asserted an aggressive position in both foreign and domestic affairs. He pursued an international policy similar to that of Theodore Roosevelt, popularized by the aphorism, "Speak softly, but carry a big stick". His political strategy remained modestly isolationist preserving neutrality, yet exercising authoritative intervention when provoked. In foreign affairs, Reagan maneuvered with diplomatic dexterity, deterring countries deemed potentially dangerous, while preserving peace with amiable nations. Such initiative successfully defeated the virulent Soviet machine, and inhibited further diffusion of Communism. Regarding domestic relations, Reagan supported a balanced limited government. He even renovated traditional federalism. Thus, Reagan advocated the democratic principles intended by our constitutional framers.

A preeminent proponent of capitalism, Reagan revitalized the sluggish U.S. economy, emphasizing supply side economics which stimulated commercial activity and suppressed inflation. To catalyze this effect, the Reagan administration minimized bureaucratic spending and superfluous tax confiscation. He sought an unregulated laissez faire strategy to corporate enterprise. Moreover, Reagan strengthened defense capability to prevent terrorism, and restored moral awareness in American culture. Furthermore, he nominated individuals who truly shared his traditional federalist values to serve as Supreme Court Judges. Thus, reshaping U.S. foreign and domestic affairs, Reagan offers an unprecedented legacy. Ronald Reagan not only revolutionized the modern presidency through various practices he standardized, consolidating national defense, restoring economic strength and military infrastructure to America, his formidable contributions prove a paragon for successors in 21st Century international politics.

Legacy of a Leader

Before Reagan entered office, American society appeared tumultuous. Torn between economic pressure and political strife, conditions seemed more than favorable for a formidable leader to emerge. Former President Jimmy Carter acted aimlessly during his single term. Politically impotent, he left America saturated in turmoil. Incapacitated and defeated, Carter departed the presidency with, "runaway inflation, gasoline shortage, and a lingering hostage crisis in Iran," (*DeGregorio – The Complete Book of U.S. Presidents, 643*). After witnessing such pervasive destruction resulting from powerless presidents, people pondered whether America's presidency might ever return to its original, "center of national consciousness which once existed between 1933 and 1973," (*Gould, The Modern American Presidency, 190*). Finally after years of tribulation and nostalgic yearnings, Ronald Reagan arrived in 1980, "reviving the modern presidency institutionally, and serving two complete terms; an achievement not pursued by any president since Dwight D. Eisenhower," (*Gould, The Modern American Presidency, 191*). His conservative brand of reconstruction revolutionized the modern presidency.

Concluding political disjunction, Reagan offered reconstruction. Prolific author Stephen Skowronek in his prominent publication, "The Politics Presidents Make" outlines the presidential patterns persistently reverberated throughout past and present American history. According to Skowronek, presidential tenure characterizes one of two phases; disjunction and reconstruction. So the pattern follows, disjunction, a period defined by decline, always precedes reconstruction. Indeed, an era denoting "disjunction" inevitably foreshadows presidential reconstruction. Why? Consider common sense application.

Any reasonable historian realizes the profound sociological impact of causation. Antecedent events inevitably cause a specific arrangement of consequences. When society witnesses decline, history facilitates the emergence of a remarkable leader to offer reconstruction. The Civil War references one example. Abraham Lincoln, a monumental leader, emerged to prominence under the most favorable circumstances, when society desperately demanded restoration. Only Lincoln possessed the quintessential qualities needed to restore prosperity in American society. The same principle applies for Ronald Reagan. Problematic circumstances necessitate reform, and history creates a context for its predestined leaders to provide such rehabilitation. The presidency repeats this same cyclical pattern throughout American history. Consider Skowronek's historical analysis regarding the tremendous sociological influence upon Ronald Reagan, particularly, how history paved his emergence as a brilliant leader.

After waiting "28 years", Republicans assembled senatorial control, dominating the disarrayed and discombobulated Democratic Party, as its administration quickly fashioned a functioning majority within Congress' House of Representatives (*Skowronek, The Politics Presidents Make, 414*). Again, the promotion of Ronald Reagan as president appeared almost inevitable. The decline of American society produced an ideal atmosphere to catalyze Reagan's emergence. Hence, history provided the most favorable conditions for a quintessential leader such as Ronald Reagan, to assert political prominence and become president. Everything happened as anticipated. Apparently, he emerged under, "circumstances that recalled the profound reconstructive crusades of America's history," (*Skowronek -*

The Politics Presidents Make, 414). President Richard Nixon said it best with the engaging assertion, "Ronald Reagan has been justified by what has happened. History has justified his leadership," (*D'Souza*, 9). The desperate demand for resolution, in combination with his magnanimity, celebrated personality, and aura of political prestige, certainly precipitated Reagan's emergence as a powerful president.

Reagan possessed a rare exceptional aptitude to connect with all kinds of diverse people among varied social status. Unlike his predecessors, who predominantly came from affluent aristocratic families, already actively involved in politics, Reagan's humble beginnings, exposed to arduous hardworking middle class conditions, endowed him with a true sense of empathy toward the American people and their struggles. Indeed, the Reagan family suffered impoverished surroundings during his childhood. However, while Reagan, "acknowledged" his family's "precarious economic status," he never perceived himself as poor since many people experienced similar circumstances, in addition to their constant humanitarian efforts, "always others less fortunate," (*D'Souza*, 38). Peggy Noonan, specialist assistant to President Reagan from 1984 to 1986, astutely described Reagan's beginnings as the "most modest and lacking of any president," within this past century (*Noonan*, 17). Fostered under such a modest environment, his childhood inculcated the invaluable quality of determination and perseverance.

Yet, as Reagan subsequently progressed in societal status, acquiring both fame and fortune, attaining prominence as a successful actor, he eventually cultivated the soft, personal skills, extroverted demeanor and etiquette highly regarded among wealthier classes. The "new money" status added a new dimension to his penetrating personality. From an allegorical perspective, Reagan represented, "a real-life Gatsby," whom F. Scott Fitzgerald recognized as exhibiting, "an extraordinary gift for hope," (*D'Souza*, 36). He combined the rigorous tough-minded strength that molded him during youth and early military service in World War II, with an urbane, smooth, attractive style, which gave roundness to his bold character. Hence, his historical lifetime experience facilitated the development of a very versatile character, one who truly understood fundamental needs concerning Americans, and the prodigious ability to empathize with their struggles. Furthermore, his indiscriminate understanding of others overcomes prejudicial barriers. Reagan truly retained unique interpersonal skills, an inherent gift refined from his personal background. Superseding societal constraints, he related to anyone from across generations.

A genuinely charismatic figure painted by his Hollywood persona and time served as Governor of California, Reagan generated instant recognition for office. Besides fame, Reagan projected a unique aura unavailable to his predecessors. His inherently vibrant versatile character, integrating unabated toughness and calm congeniality quelled even the harshest of opponents. He combined callous resistance with kind candor, while simultaneously juxtaposing intellectual sharpness and soft charm in synergistic blend. Humorous yet authoritative, ordinary though heroic, individual nonetheless representative, Reagan "embodied a sonorous, multidimensional character; one that transcended Kennedy in mythic resonance," (*Nelson –The Presidency and the Political System*, 301).

Reagan naturally blended joviality with authority, expressing a warm grin, "to remove any intimations of callousness," (*Nelson –The Presidency and the Political System*, 301). Thus, he disguised his innate aggressiveness with wittiness, usually followed by a, "characteristically clever one-liner," (*Nelson –The Presidency and the Political System*, 301). Also, his prolific masculine image, as portrayed prospered. The American people instantly saw an indefatigable crusader, that even at age seventy, "rode horses, exercised vigorously, and commonly identified himself with Clint Eastwood or Sylvester Stallone among celebrity tough guys," (*Nelson –The Presidency and the Political System*, 301).

Those who personally knew Reagan regarded him as a sanguine individual, both, "even-tempered, and forever optimistic," (*DeGregorio –*

The Complete Book of U.S. Presidents, 634). He possessed a mesmerizing attractiveness, capable of hypnotizing anyone, including leftists. For this reason, some deemed him much more politically moderate than appeared true. Even the liberal *New York Times* once stipulated that, "his aw-shucks manner and charming good looks disarm those who distantly perceive him as a far right fanatic," (H. Smith, "*Reagan: The Man, The President.*" 152).

Interestingly, Reagan experienced an ideological metamorphosis in political affiliation, further supplementing the highly attractive, relatively moderate appeal attributed to his character. For example, following the liberal traditions inculcated by his father Jack Reagan, Ronald originally initiated himself politically as a Democrat. After returning from World War II as Captain and reserve cavalry officer, he voted for Franklin D. Roosevelt in 1932, supporting the New Deal. When Reagan returned to Warner Brothers in Hollywood, he joined, "the left leaning American Veterans Committee" and served as a committee board constituent for Hollywood Independent Citizens Committee of Arts (Evans, 6). However, he later delivered presidential speeches for Harry Truman and even, "campaigned in support of Helen Gahagan Douglas, who ran as senator against Richard Nixon," (*DeGregorio – The Complete Book of U.S. Presidents, 641*). By this time, Reagan progressively became a staunch social and fiscal conservative.

As President of the Screen Actors Guild, Reagan pursued a career that ultimately preordained his direction into politics. Elected twice, his tenure lasted from 1947-1960. On October 23, 1947, Reagan testified as witness before the *House Un-American Activities Committee* (HUAC) against communism, and secretly reported any actions of American disloyalty, to the FBI under the code name "Agent T-10" (*Reagan, 1947 HUAC testimony*, 1). Reagan also exhibited no reluctance toward blacklisting. Ironically, private documents reveal that Reagan supposedly condemned the unnecessary, "witch hunting tactics Congress imposed in conducting its investigation," (*DeGregorio – The Complete Book of U.S. Presidents, 641*).

In the 1948 presidential election, still registered as a Democrat, Reagan solicited tremendous support, campaigning for Harry Truman (*Encyclopedia Britannica Profiles – The American Presidency, Ronald Reagan,* 1). Then in the fifties and most especially early sixties, Reagan officially converted to conservatism. His allegiance to the Democratic Party ended in 1952 (*American National Biography Online,* 2). The Republican Party appeared more compatible with his newly adopted conservative values. Identifying the Republicans as more considerably capable of combating communism, he gradually abandoned his left-leanings, supporting the presidential candidacies of Dwight Eisenhower from 1952-56 and then Richard Nixon in 1960. In 1962, Reagan formally registered himself a Republican and began to campaign for Barry Goldwater two years later. He drastically transformed, "from the near hopeless hemophiliac liberal who bled for causes, to an ardently conservative Republican," (*DeGregorio – The Complete Book of U.S. Presidents, 641*).

Several motivational factors account for Reagan's ideological metamorphosis. By the 1950s, communism emerged to fruition, caused considerable concern. At an impressionable age, after finishing his military service in World War II, Reagan seemed reluctantly susceptible to the ambivalent political environment evolving during that era. As Noonan verbatim asserts, "Reagan was trying to remain a liberal at a moment when it seemed to him that liberals had gone blind," (Noonan, 60). Communism heightened apprehension as it permeated the international landscape. To America, witnessing its destructive imperialistic influence posed by Joseph Stalin, communism surfaced as the driving force of fear, an imminent threat targeting U.S. interests. Hence, the Cold War, a cultural war analogous to America's contemporary War against Terror, commenced, in its preliminary premature phase of development. Fear served as the impetus of ideological transition, inculcating a rather reactionary response in American perception. The wave of McCarthyism and conservative sentiment served as a national defense mechanism to preserve authoritative order, in protection against communist virulence.

Consequently, since communism proved a direct threat to U.S. interests, impassioned conservatism surfaced in the mindset of mainstream Americans. As Americans feared that communism threatened its conventional constitutional values, the strong capitalistic spirit and democratic fervor representing our national heritage, conservatism dominated American perception. Reagan, a true advocate of American democracy, passionate and patriotic, remained predisposed to this proud attitude, affirming the libertarian values founded by our constitutional framers. Reagan and several other similar-minded actors collectively participating in the de Haviland group promulgated a statement of policy reflecting such principles, which announced, "We reaffirm our belief in free enterprise and the democratic system and repudiate communism as desirable for the United States," (Noonan, 59).

By now, Reagan maintained a moderate posture in politics. Again, he condemned the leftist propagandist platform endorsed by Hollywood, and their soft passive position concerning communism, yet eschewed such "wrongful" accusations that portrayed certain individuals as "communists" just because they espoused liberalism (Noonan, 64). Even so, from Reagan's perspective, he retained the same central "basic values" he always favored, solid commitment to democratic principle, and thus never underwent, "any radical [ideological] transformation," (Noonan, 60). So, whether conservative or liberal, Reagan believed in the promise of democratic freedom. However, he soon began to realize the unrealistic, naïve approach of traditional liberal doctrine in America.

Even some good liberals, individuals who favor democratic principles, passively acquiesced to communism. Predominantly supporting its socialistic orientation, they embraced such egalitarian interests, advocating social welfare for destitute Americans, at the unfortunate detrimental expense of capitalistic opportunity. Thus, young Reagan, a political moderate espousing many liberal beliefs, felt totally out of place in this ambivalent climate caught between two ideological extremes. Conversely, the extreme leftists, especially many Hollywood celebrities, with their subversive disposition, sought communist takeover. Indeed, they shared the views of Vladimir Lenin, pushing for an international revolution, subsumed and subjugated by communist oppression. Therefore, during a vulnerable uncertain period in U.S. history, endangered by communism, the earliest manifestations of Cold War tensions stimulated conservative reaction, which perhaps explains one factor influencing Ronald Reagan and his ideological transition to traditional American conservatism. The historical climate in America encouraged Reagan's ideological transition. His conservative awakening only began to materialize. Yet, other contributing reasons account for this transition.

Many people often neglect the profound ideological impact of Ronald's wife, Nancy Reagan, fostered in a conventional conservative environment, reinforced by commitment to abundant family traditions. Raised in the conservative tradition, Nancy obviously wielded profound influence upon Reagan's ideological interpretation and political perspective. Like Abigail Adams, Eleanor Roosevelt, among other strong women throughout American history, Nancy Reagan assumed an aggressive role in her husband's presidential policy. She exercised tremendous influence regarding various and sundry personal issues. Ultimately, Nancy not only played a pivotal role in Ronald Reagan's ideological transition, but asserted active administrative involvement throughout his presidential tenure. The preeminent "politician's wife", Nancy's tenacity to tackle "tough measures" and prevent anyone from undermining his reputation, because she understood her "role very well," proved an invaluable utility (D'Souza, 221, 32).

Few people examine his 'conversion to conservatism' better than Thomas Evans, attorney and former chair of the Reagan administration's national symposium on partnerships in education. In his distinguished book, "The Education of Ronald Reagan - The General Electric Years and the Untold Story of his Conversion to Conservatism" Evans documents the personal struggles Reagan endured during his dramatic ideological transformation from liberal to conservative. For example, the 1946 strike, perhaps, "the greatest year of strike activity since 1919," as one labor historian concluded, caused serious repercussions that compelled Reagan to rethink his political philosophy (Evans, 34).

According to D'Szoua, "when Reagan travelled the country for General Electric," he soon recognized political usurpation, "a degree of government intrusion in people's lives that threatened their fundamental liberties," (D'Souza, 60). He witnessed the democratic violations that deprived good Americans of the individual freedom guaranteed by our constitutional foundation, through his participation in GE. Thomas Evans shared this same mutual consensus with Dinesh D' Souza. However, Evans delves one step further. The strike exercised tremendous sociological influence upon Reagan's political perception.

As Evans asserts, "dealing with the intersection of long-range goals and immediate, unexpected crises occurring on a number of independent fronts – presented a unique opportunity to learn, one that few men and women," in public office ever experience (Evans, 127). Reagan received the honorary privilege to prosper in knowledge, facilitating his intellectual advancement. He assimilated insight not ordinarily available to persons in his position, associating with prominent individuals, particularly Lemuel Boulware and Laurence Beilenson, who stimulated Reagan's personal enlightenment. Therefore, Evans references the educational context that facilitated Reagan's conversion to conservatism, through his participation in G.E.

Ronald Reagan's superior postgraduate education while representing General Electric, experiencing the aesthetic beauty of American corporate initiative and capitalistic spirit, profoundly influenced his political perspective concerning democratic opportunity. Hence, he soon developed a sincere appreciation for private business. Assuming position of student, Reagan learned extensively from his role model and political mentor, the highly influential Lemuel Boulware.

Under the guiding tutelage of Boulware, Reagan in time cultivated scholarly erudition. Established in 1956, the General Electric Company, located at Ossining, New York, offered a formidable educational facility, with its own independent, "learning center and recreation building," (Evans, 69). It accommodated, "more students, 32,000, than most universities," (*Time*, 76). Here, Reagan acquired access to, "lessons and texts," that specifically provided powerful pedagogical resources for "middle management" workers of the company (Evans, 69). Reagan developed a sophisticated understanding of the U.S. economic system, which proved instrumental to his subsequent conservative fiscal policy strategy as president. Reagan later recalls his transformational, "post-graduate education in political science," and, "apprenticeship for public life," paving the road to his political prominence (Evans, 38). Moreover, he established sincere camaraderie and, "rapport with General Electric" employees, invaluable connections that benefitted him overwhelmingly in upcoming years (Evans, 113).

Evans demonstrates that Boulware, conspicuous spokesperson for GE, played a pivotal role in the political transformation of Ronald Reagan. A notable individual, or "manager extraordinaire" as Evans describes, Boulware, regarded among, "the most influential executives," emerged to leadership in General Electric, teaching political economics (Evans, 38). He believed education an invaluable and indispensable element to economic prosperity.

With compelling conviction, Boulware influenced employees. In one particular speech, pontificating before his students, he articulated, "… incredible achievements to show for our management of the business side of our wonderful system of freedoms, incentives, and competition…," (Evans, 42). Like Adam Smith, Boulware championed corporate opportunity, inculcating such lofty capitalistic values into workers. Boulware condemned the socialistic oriented union institutions that undermined and disparaged free enterprise. Envision the tenacity of this gentleman. Boulware not only wanted businessmen to ameliorate their personal reputation, he desired that they become engrossed in, "process of conveying his messages," (Evans, 43). Therefore, Lemuel Boulware deserves partial credit to the innovative genius of Reaganomics, which Reagan subsequently grandfathered as his brainchild.

Boulware facilitated the foundation of conservatism for Ronald Reagan. Reagan and Boulware worked in "close proximity" for seven years, assuming the relationship role of "mentorship" (Evan, 11). Here, Reagan became exposed to the destructive nature pervading avaricious labor unions, challenging his dogmatic liberal beliefs, preconceived views he harbored since early childhood. Reagan soon witnessed the liberal degradation of society demoralizing American democracy, corrupting public school curricula, and imposing repressive, "welfare programs," which exacerbated crime (*American National Biography*, 3). Through Bouleware, Reagan derived a savvy sophisticated understanding of the American economic system, which catalyzed his conversion to conservatism. Boulware maintained two principal components incorporated by Reagan during his presidential tenure. First, he advocated "an ideology" that specifically outlined the prototypical ideal for America. Secondly, Boulware introduced a "methodology" that prescribed how to attain these aspirations (Evan, 38).

Another influential figure, Laurence Beilenson, Reagan's esteemed attorney, contributed considerably to his conservative conversion. Evans specifically alludes to Beilenson regarding his personal impact upon Reagan's unmistakable 1964 speech, presently known as "The Speech". According to Evans, Beilenson exercised a direct unambiguous influence upon Reagan's international relations. Evans believes that Beilenson, "more than Boulware" or "anyone else" shaped Reagan's political perceptions regarding foreign policy (Evan, 116). Evans elaborates even further inferring that Beilenson's insight ultimately facilitated "establishment of the Reagan Doctrine", helped conclude "America's containment policy with Soviet Russia," and contributed to endorse, "a nuclear- defense shield," in subsequent years when Reagan became president (Evans, 116). These concepts introduce the conservative foreign policy strategy originated by Ronald Reagan. Expect further exploration of the aforementioned topics in latter discussion.

The respectable attorney first received recognition representing SAG. Obviously, Reagan later summoned his expert legal consultation, as a connoisseur of international law, to administer presidential foreign policy initiative. Beilenson gave Reagan a coherent framework to follow. Perhaps Evans exaggerates the notable external influence of Boulware and Beilenson upon Reagan's presidential management. Nevertheless, such evidence elucidates a clearer, more historically accurate portrait of Ronald Reagan, as the unparalleled crusader who harnessed his formidable education, voluminous knowledge, and veteran experience influenced by other incandescent minds, to rehabilitate American society, more specifically, conquering communism, while simultaneously regenerating sound economic policy.

Once again, history produced the emergence of Reagan, inevitably foreshadowed by his fate as an extraordinary leader. Reagan combined the collective genius of others, assimilating their profound intellect to construct an intelligent, creatively designed administrative platform that delivered efficient political policy. As historical scholar John Sloan acknowledged, Reagan's, "effectiveness of leadership" remained predicated upon his unprecedented ability to solicit and exploit the talents exemplified by, "conservatives, pragmatists, and public relations experts," (Sloan, John, x).

Reagan gradually began to adopt the central intrinsic tenets of modern American fiscal conservatism. Such conservative values included solid dedication to anticommunism, reduced taxes, and a balanced limited government, which Reagan developed through his active participation in General Electric. Again, Boulware became the catalyst to Reagan's ideological transition. As Reagan himself professed in relation to his extensive G.E. tours,

> "...I was seeing how government really operated and affected people in America, not how it was taught in school...how the ever-expanding government was encroaching on liberties we'd always taken for granted...," (*Reagan,* An American Life, 129).

This evolutionary transition to conservatism occurred over a span of "eight years", serving his leadership in the Employee and Community Relations Program, assigned by Boulware (Evan, 11). Between 1954 and 1962, Reagan conspicuously established himself as a conservative. Indeed, Reagan's subsequent speeches substantially reflected the conservative sentiments, even grandiloquent language expressed by Boulware.

According to Evans, Reagan's famous 1964 presentation, "The Speech" closely resembled the remarks of a message delivered by Lem Boulware, "on June 11, 1949," which addressed, "graduate students and alumni at Harvard Business School," (Evans, 40). Moreover, as Evans continues, "Boulware's language "came much closer to "The Speech" than Reagan's America the Beautiful," delivered in 1952 at a William Woods College commencement ceremony, invited by Dr. Raymond McCallister, Protestant minister from St. Louis (Evans, 40, 16). The monumental 1964 speech represents a byproduct of Reagan's conservative foundation cultivated during his propitious professional experience with General Electric. His conversion to conservatism finally witnessed fullest effect.

In 1964, during his final week, "serving as cochairman of California Republicans for Goldwater, he delivered a 30-minute television address that even the *New York Times* glorified as it, "drew more contributions than any other political speech throughout history," (Barnes, 1, *Washington Post*). Reagan presented the original ideas extracted from Boulware, in a characteristically innovative, insightful manner that demonstrated his individual application of solid, regimented education. Entitled, "A Time for Choosing" Reagan referenced his true political position, as a consummate crusader of American democracy, defending our great founding fathers, and the unsurpassed freedom they intended for Americans. Here, Reagan enumerated the flaws of big bureaucratic government, condemning superfluous taxation without representation, inordinate political expenditures, unnecessary welfare programs, passive liberal acquiescence to communist sentiment, and most importantly, dangers surrounding partisanship. Again, Boulwarism, as it subsequently became known, manifested its presence, reverberating throughout the speech. Reagan emphasized the teachings of Boulware as his central theme, to address ordinary Americans.

Reagan declared the significance of government accountability, a responsibility retained by our constitutional founders to preserve liberty, freedom, and authoritative order. During the speech, Reagan advocated strong capitalist initiative, and reiterated the importance of promoting the unrivaled equal corporate opportunity guaranteed to America by our Constitutional framers. He also plainly discussed on a practical level, the threat to freedom, and oppressive environment facing everyday Americans in their ordinary lives, resulting from fiscal irresponsibility. Consider the following excerpt. Reagan delivered a powerful message that empathized with every citizen on all levels. Hence, on October 27, 1964, in his poignant proclamation, Reagan verbatim promulgated,

> "… Those who deplore use of the terms "pink" and "leftist" are themselves guilty of branding all who oppose their liberalism as right wing extremists. How long can we afford the luxury of this family fight when we are at war with the most dangerous enemy ever known to man?...If freedom is lost here there is no place to escape to…
>
> …It's time we asked ourselves if we still know the freedoms intended for us by the Founding Fathers. James Madison said, "We base all our experiments on the capacity of mankind for self-government." This idea that government was beholden to the people, that it had no

other source of power except the sovereign people, is still the newest, most unique idea in all the long history of man's relation to man. For almost two centuries we have proved man's capacity for self-government, but today we are told we must choose between a left and right or, as others suggest, a third alternative, a kind of safe middle ground. I suggest to you there is no left or right, only an up or down. Up to the maximum of individual freedom consistent with law and order, or down to the ant heap of totalitarianism; and regardless of their humanitarian purpose those who would sacrifice freedom for security have, whether they know it or not, chosen this downward path. Plutarch warned, "The real destroyer of the liberties of the people is he who spreads among them bounties, donations, and benefits…

…Another articulate spokesman for the welfare state defines liberalism as meeting the material needs of the masses through the full power of centralized government. I for one find it disturbing when a representative refers to the free men and women of this country as the masses, but beyond this the full power of centralized government was the very thing the Founding Fathers sought to minimize. They knew you don't control things; you can't control the economy without controlling people. So we have come to a time for choosing. Either we accept the responsibility for our own destiny, or we abandon the American Revolution and confess that an intellectual belief in a far-distant capitol can plan our lives for us better than we can plan them ourselves…

Government has laid its hand on health, housing, farming, industry, commerce, education, and, to an ever-increasing degree, interferes with the people's right to know. Government tends to grow; government programs take on weight and momentum, as public servants say, always with the best of intentions, "What greater service we could render if only we had a little more money and a little more power." But the truth is that outside of its legitimate function, government does nothing as well or as economically as the private sector of the economy…The specter our well-meaning liberal friends refuse to face is that their policy of accommodation is appeasement, and appeasement does not give you a choice between peace and war, only between fight and surrender. We are told that the problem is too complex for a simple answer. They are wrong…We must have the courage to do what we know is morally right, and this policy of accommodation asks us to accept the greatest possible immorality. We are being asked to buy our safety from the threat of "the bomb" by selling into permanent slavery our fellow human beings enslaved behind the Iron Curtain, to tell them to give up their hope of freedom because we are ready to make a deal with their slave masters.

Alexander Hamilton warned us that a nation which can prefer disgrace to danger is prepared for a master and deserves one. Admittedly there is a risk in any course we follow. Choosing the high road cannot eliminate that risk. Already some of the architects of accommodation have hinted what their decision will be if their plan fails and we are faced with the final ultimatum…Should Moses have told the children of Israel to live in slavery rather than dare the wilderness? Should Christ have refused the Cross? Should the patriots at Concord Bridge have refused to fire the shot heard 'round the world? Are we to believe that all the martyrs of history died in vain?

…We can preserve for our children this, the last best hope of man on earth, or we can sentence them to take the first step into a thousand years of darkness. If we fail, at least let our children and our children's children say of us we justified our brief moment here. We did all that could be done." (Reagan Library, "A Time For Choosing").

By the time of his presidency, Reagan already succeeded in establishing himself as the prototypical American icon. Election Day, Nov 4, 1981, proved an indisputable victory. The people ultimately distinguished Reagan as a prominent leader, earning, "489 total combined electoral votes in all but six states," (Biography of Ronald Reagan, 1). Overtime, Reagan's popularity only flourished. Upon re-election, Reagan finished with 59% of the popular vote and received a remarkable 525 electoral votes, constituting, "the most total electoral votes in history," (*DeGregorio – The Complete Book of U.S. Presidents, 646*).

In addition to popularity, *The Great Communicator*, institutionalized various standards for his successors. For example, succinct radio addresses, or "the president's weekly radio address" as presently called, appeared naturally every Saturday morning, becoming "an indelible part of the nation's political landscape," (*Gould, The Modern American Presidency, 194*). Also, The State of the Union Address achieved new show business aspects under Ronald Reagan. Unlike previous televised renderings of a president communicating to Congress, Reagan delivered presentations that incorporated, "heroes, distinguished Americans, and individuals who demonstrated policy needs, among various guests sitting in the visitor's gallery," (*Gould – The Modern American Presidency, 195*). Moreover, State of the Union Addresses featured a very theatrical appearance. With time, "even state governors started emulating the techniques employed by Reagan in their locally televised State of the State addresses," (*Gould – The Modern American Presidency, 195*).

On January 26, 1982, Reagan presented his first presidential State of the Union Address before Congress. Reagan deemed it a constitutional obligation to secure the freedom, liberty, and pursuit of happiness for all citizens, as championed by our founding fathers. Proclaiming his faith in the fairness and general welfare of Americans, Reagan expresses venerable dedication to those democratic values, as a constitutional duty. In this excerpt Reagan references his consummate commitment to American democracy.

"...Today marks my first State of the Union address to you, a constitutional duty as old as our Republic itself...

President Washington began this tradition in 1790 after reminding the Nation that the destiny of self-government and the ``preservation of the sacred fire of liberty" is ``finally staked on the experiment entrusted to the hands of the American people." For our friends in the press, who place a high premium on accuracy, let me say: I did not actually hear George Washington say that...But it is a matter of historic record...

...But from this podium, Winston Churchill asked the free world to stand together against the onslaught of aggression. Franklin Delano Roosevelt spoke of a day of infamy and summoned a nation to arms. Douglas MacArthur made an unforgettable farewell to a country he loved and served so well. Dwight Eisenhower reminded us that peace was purchased only at the price of strength. And John F. Kennedy spoke of the burden and glory that is freedom...

...In forging this new partnership for America, we could achieve the oldest hopes of our Republic -- prosperity for our nation, peace for the world, and the blessings of individual liberty for our children and, someday, for all of humanity...

...It's my duty to report to you tonight...on the foundation we've carefully laid for our economic recovery, and finally, on a bold and spirited initiative that I believe can change the face of American government and make it again the servant of the people. ...we as Americans have the capacity now, as we've had it in the past, to do whatever needs to be done to preserve this last and greatest bastion of freedom."...

... Tonight I'm urging the American people: Seize these new opportunities to produce, to save, to invest, and together we'll make this economy a mighty engine of freedom, hope, and prosperity again...

...We'll continue to redirect our resources to our two highest budget priorities -- a strong national defense to keep America free and at peace and a reliable safety net of social programs for those who have contributed and those who are in need...

...Waste and fraud are serious problems. Back in 1980 Federal investigators testified before one of your committees that ``corruption has permeated virtually every area of the Medicare and Medicaid health care industry." ... I ask you to help make these savings for the American taxpayer... I am confident the economic program we've put into operation will protect the needy while it triggers a recovery that will benefit all Americans...Now that the essentials of that program are in place, our next major undertaking must be a program -- just as bold, just as innovative -- to make government again accountable to the people, to make our system of federalism work again...

...The growth in these Federal programs has -- in the words of one intergovernmental commission -- made the Federal Government ``more pervasive, more intrusive, more unmanageable, more ineffective and costly, and above all, more [un]accountable."

...This administration has faith in State and local governments and the constitutional balance envisioned by the Founding Fathers. We also believe in the integrity, decency, and sound, good sense of grassroots Americans.

...Our nation's long journey towards civil rights for all our citizens -- once a source of discord, now a source of pride -- must continue with no backsliding or slowing down. We must and shall see that those basic laws that guarantee equal rights are preserved and, when necessary, strengthened.

Our concern for equal rights for women is firm and unshakable. We launched a new Task Force on Legal Equity for Women and a Fifty States Project that will examine State laws for discriminatory language. And for the first time in our history, a woman sits on the highest court in the land...

...Our foreign policy is a policy of strength, fairness, and balance. By restoring America's military credibility, by pursuing peace at the negotiating table wherever both sides are willing to sit down in good faith, and by regaining the respect of America's allies and adversaries alike, we have strengthened our country's position as a force for peace and progress in the world...

When action is called for, we're taking it. Our sanctions against the military dictatorship that has attempted to crush human rights in Poland -- and against the Soviet regime behind that military dictatorship -- clearly demonstrated to the world that America will not conduct ``business as usual'' with the forces of oppression.

...In the face of a climate of falsehood and misinformation, we've promised the world a season of truth -- the truth of our great civilized ideas: individual liberty, representative government, the rule of law under God. ..

...A hundred and twenty years ago, the greatest of all our Presidents delivered his second State of the Union message in this Chamber. ``We cannot escape history,'' Abraham Lincoln warned. ``We of this Congress and this administration will be remembered in spite of ourselves.'' The ``trial through which we pass will light us down, in honor or dishonor, to the latest [last] generation.'' ...

...Well, that President and that Congress did not fail the American people. Together they weathered the storm and preserved the Union. Let it be said of us that

> we, too, did not fail; that we, too, worked together to bring America through difficult times. Let us so conduct ourselves that two centuries from now, another Congress and another President, meeting in this Chamber as we are meeting, will speak of us with pride, saying that we met the test and preserved for them in their day the sacred flame of liberty -- this last, best hope of man on Earth. God bless you, and thank you," (Reagan Presidential Library, First State of the Union Address, 1).

Reagan opened his speech recalling the prophetic words pronounced by George Washington, preserving, "the fire of liberty," a voracious passion our constitutional founders vehemently defended, (Reagan Presidential Library, First State of the Union Address, 1). Reagan reiterates this allegorical "flame of liberty," to suggest its sacred nature and aesthetic quality, the delicate beauty derived from freedom, a firm though fragile gift which requires tremendous tender care. Freedom extrapolates its formidable strength from the fervent dedication people furnish to preserve it. Such freedom, as Washington proclaimed rests solely with, "the American people," (Reagan Presidential Library, First State of the Union Address, 1).

Reagan accentuated these words to elucidate the significance of both our moral and constitutional duty. Ronald Reagan, more than any modern president, understood, in totality, the intentions of our constitutional founders, as he proclaims, "...In forging this new partnership for America, we could achieve the oldest hopes of our Republic -- prosperity for our nation, peace for the world, and the blessings of individual liberty for our children and, someday, for all of humanity...," (Reagan Presidential Library, First State of the Union Address, 1).

His words resurrect the Declaration of Independence, as Adams, Franklin, and Jefferson professed, advocating that all people possess certain inherent "inalienable rights" guaranteed by their Creator. Reagan also outlined the severe flaws of federal programs, discussing its predisposition to usurpation. Reagan recognized the egalitarian concept of equality as conceived by our constitutional founders. He condemned the lack of "accountability" exercised by government, castigating administrative incompetence and imprudent decisions undermining American democracy. He also discussed accountability in terms of entrepreneurial "innovation", introducing effective, creative policy initiatives, to reinvigorate federalism as explicitly enumerated by the U.S. Constitution. Likewise, Reagan emphasized the paramount significance of government responsibility, by additionally alluding to Lincoln's second State of the Union Address. Again, Reagan demonstrates his sincerest dedication to libertarian democratic values.

Thus, from Reagan's view, the preeminent proponent of modern American democracy, individual liberty represented a ubiquitous blessing not exclusively shared by Americans, but applies universally, entitled to everyone everywhere. To him, American hegemony served as a paragon for other nations, the quintessential paradigm of democratic freedom. Reagan utilized his character and sage words of wisdom to embody this theme, eventually becoming the aspiring legacy he advocated; a paragon for subsequent government leaders. Ultimately, he instituted the standard, an example for others to follow, restoring democratic peace, prosperity, and stability in society.

Reagan fulfilled the prophecy, though transient, at least for a temporary period, containing, and eventually conquering communism, thereby ensuring international tranquility. Reagan promised to strengthen military infrastructure, exercising authoritative force, while contemporaneously establishing diplomatic alliance with supportive nations, providing protection against any totalitarian threat, particularly Soviet Communism, which he indeed accomplished. The Reagan administration superseded Soviet expenditure, producing voluminous accumulation of nuclear capability, exacerbated by Gorbachev himself, in his feeble attempt to reform a hopelessly unchangeable regime. Ultimately, Reagan "bankrupted the Soviet Union" through its relentless arms race, catalyzing its self-destruction (Friedman, Thomas, 55).

Moreover, notice how Reagan affirmed his dedication to Americans indiscriminately, without class distinction, addressing the needs of Americans. He explicitly promised never to abandon the "poor and elderly". President Reagan accentuated the corruption pervading, "virtually every area of the Medicare and Medicaid health care industry," (Reagan Presidential Library, First State of the Union Address, 1). Again, Reagan harnessed his own personal experience to accommodate the needs and interests of Americans. He truly understood the plight and predicament surrounding destitute communities across America. Therefore, he deliberately sought, as a principal initiative, to ameliorate conditions for impoverished and elderly Americans.

He related to everyone, superseding class boundaries. Reagan announced his primary objective as President, "... a bold and spirited initiative that I believe can change the face of American government and make it again the servant of the people...," (Reagan Presidential Library, First State of the Union Address, 1). Yet, unlike other conservative presidents who relied on false hopes and empty promises, Reagan remained true to the principles he advocated. Most presidents summon a ghostwriter to compose their speech. Not Reagan. President Reagan admitted in his own personal journal that he wrote the State of the Union Address before "leaving for the Capitol" (*Reagan, Brinkley*, 65). Therefore, Ronald Reagan elevated the presidential State of the Union Address to new heights, offering never before seen depth and dimension.

Furthermore, another innovative tradition which assimilated into the presidency under Reagan involved this concept of scheduling the President's day to accommodate news cycle and network television coverage. The media proved a powerful instrument for Reagan to structure his presentations. Already comfortable performing from a daily shooting schedule the beforehand preparation of an agenda that outlined his daily events, proved reassuring for him. He thoroughly understood the value of repetition and extemporaneous speech. Including every detail, he delivered his presentation, "with practiced professionalism, moving seamlessly through routines, possessing the skill of a star who realizes that production results depend on competence and reliability," (*Gould – The Modern American Presidency, 195*). Even inflammatory critics recognized Reagan's compelling conviction as a grandiloquent communicator, one whose, "theatrical and oratory skills kept his countrymen spellbound and cheering," (*D'Souza*, 11).

Once elected, Reagan immediately took charge. Again, conditions heretofore seemed discombobulated, the situation in disarray. However, ambivalence imminently dissipated when Ronald Reagan entered the presidency. From the beginning, President Reagan automatically understood his role as Chief Executive. Since then, American society only flourished. Demonstrating diplomatic dexterity, he exploited, "the political momentum of his landslide victory and the wave of national sympathy after an attempted assassination, to initiate tax reduction," (*Gould – The Modern American Presidency, 198*).

On "March 30, 1981", John Hinckley attempted to target a malevolent murder against President Ronald Reagan (Alderman, Kennedy, 93). It all happened as Reagan departed the Washington Hilton Hotel. This occurred only "69 days" after his inauguration (Net127, 1). The 25 year old lunatic fired six successive shots, "Devastator explosive rounds", with a ".22 Rohm RG-14 Revolver" at President Reagan severely wounding Press Secretary James Brady, Secret Service agent Timothy McCarthy, and policeman Thomas Delahanty (*DeGregorio – The Complete Book of U.S. Presidents, 651*). One shot penetrated Brady's head, leaving him permanently paralyzed (*Sloan, The Reagan Effect…*, 127). Reagan endured several shots that collapsed his lungs. Another bullet became lodged, landing approximately one inch from his heart (*Simon & Schuster*, "Ronald Reagan Assassination Attempt, 1).

Ironically, this attempted assassination heinously perpetrated by Hinckley remained impertinent to political association. Indeed, many people tend to carry the preconceived notion that Reagan served as President, "for years," before his attempted assassination, when meanwhile, it happened within, "a matter of nine weeks," (*Noonan*, 173). Furthermore, people naturally expect such an assassination to reference political motivation, or some ingrained hatred toward the president, as with Lincoln, McKinley, and Kennedy.

Rather, Hinckley, a deeply deranged psychopath, disturbed and depraved, obsessively infatuated with Jodi Foster, unleashed his sadistic sexual fantasies, intending to supposedly prove his insane love for her, through the reprehensible assassination attempt against President Reagan. As Reagan himself recalls, "…for some reason Hinckley decided to get a gun and kill somebody to demonstrate his love for the actress (*Reagan, Ronald*, "Reagan, An American Life", 263). Hinckley ostensibly associates his assassination attempt with intent to impress Foster. Hinckley verbatim affirmed his reason for targeting the President in a letter addressed to Jodie Foster, claiming,

> "There is a definite possibility that I will be killed in my attempt to get Reagan. It is for this very reason that I am writing you this letter now…Jodie, I would abandon this idea of getting Reagan in a second if I could only win your heart and live out the rest of my life with you, whether it be in total obscurity or whatever. I will admit to you that the reason I'm going ahead with this attempt now is because I just cannot wait any longer to impress you. I've got to do something now to make you understand, in no uncertain terms, that I am doing all of this for your sake! By sacrificing my freedom and possibly my life, I hope to change your mind about me…," (Linder, Doug, 1).

Hinckley documents an extensive history of psychosis. His actions seem to practically parallel the storyline of hit movie "Taxi Driver" featuring both Jodie Foster and Robert De Niro. Hinckley's psychiatrists overwhelmingly concluded his delusional mental state. At trial, Psychiatrist William Carpenter from the University of Maryland testified that Hinckley descended into, "'process' schizophrenia", expressing an, "incapacity" to experience, "ordinary emotional arousal associated with events in life," (CourtTV, Crime Library, 8 "The John Hinckley Case").

The attempted assassination introduced several laws. This historical incident holds monumental significance because it revolutionized

American law, legal procedure, and judicial interpretation. For example, in 1994, Congress proposed the Brady Hand Gun Violence Prevention Act, sanctioned by President Bill Clinton, named after James Brady, shot and severely wounded during Hinckley's assassination attempt on Reagan.

The Brady Hand Gun Law mandated, "a five day" delay period preceding purchase of any handgun, and most importantly, established, "instant criminal background check system" requiring gun dealers to scrutinize purchaser identity, corroborating valid I.D. such as driver's license (Schmalleger, 66). Secondly, the law attempted to ensure that only responsible individuals obtain possession of a handgun, requiring purchaser application, preventing potential federal, state, and local law violations (Schmalleger, 66). This significant statute, though still severely flawed in its application, proved an innovative measure to deter crime, and ensure that only responsible lawful citizens acquire handgun possession.

In terms of trial procedure, the Hinckley incident introduced an Insanity Defense accompanied by scathing social reaction. Hinckley received acquittal on the grounds of "severe delusions" and "schizophrenia" claiming diminished capacity resulting from an irresistible impulse or volitional incapacity, unable to control his actions, as stipulated by defense attorneys (Schmalleger, 146). According to defense, under contemporary Model Penal Code Law, Hinckley lacked sufficient mens rea, a malevolent intent or motivation for his attempted murder, and thereby ostensibly justifies insanity.

The decision fomented inflammatory hostility among many disconcerted mainstream Americans, discontent with what they perceived as an unreasonable injustice. Indeed, the verdict remains unjustifiable. How unconscionable! Hinckley still intended to murder Reagan as a means of proving his sick sadistic love for Foster. Whether or not he possessed hatred for Reagan remains impertinent to the point. He still referenced an unquestionable motivation to assassinate, and therefore sufficiently satisfies criminal intent. Nevertheless, the incident signifies a revolutionary historical development in legal reform, for which Ronald Reagan deserves credit. Ironically, the unanticipated consequences of history trigger remarkable sociological development in society.

Fortunately, Reagan survived the severe impact. Reagan represents, "the first president to survive any wound," resulting from an assassination attempt (*D'Souza*, 206). His resolute courage, resilience and unrelenting determination, despite the trauma, not only paved significant public sympathy, but rather proved the presidential strength of Ronald Reagan as a remarkable leader. As D'Souza most accurately assessed, "...The assassination attempt showed...that his spirit remained intact... [giving] the President an almost mythic dimension in the eyes of his countrymen," (*D'Souza*, 207). It undoubtedly remains a testament to his unrivaled character. In the hospital, Reagan wrote,

> "I opened my eyes once to find Nancy there...God has blessed me giving her to me is the greatest and beyond anything I can ever hope to deserve," (Brinkley, Reagan, xi).

However, marginal political embellishment perhaps contributed at least partially to positive public perception. As Sloan astutely observes "Reagan's efforts" received recognition only after the shooting, since this "near tragedy of a life-threatening gunshot wound," generated , "universally acclaimed triumph by his skilled public relations staff," (*Sloan, The Reagan Effect...*, 126). After all, Reagan's disapproval rating remained abominable, retaining "24%" which Samuel Kernell identified as, "the lowest approve-to-disapprove ratio" historically recorded by Gallup, "for a president within his second month in office," (Kernell, Samuel, 126).

Unquestionably, the assassination buttressed presidential support. Consequently, after the futile assassination attempt, Reagan's approval rating suddenly skyrocketed, "7 points," while disapproval numbers deflated by "6" (Edwards III, George, Gallup, Alec M., 91). Nevertheless,

Reagan naturally gathered the necessary public sympathy accorded to anyone encountering similar conditions, yet with diplomatic dexterity, exploited it as an effective political stratagem that promoted his economic program, which proved subsequently advantageous concerning U.S. domestic interests. Ultimately, the U.S. economy prospered.

Thus, in response, Reagan proposed a formidable tax cut program designed to refurbish economic prosperity. On April 28, 1981, President Reagan delivered his first speech after the assassination attempt. Addressing the Economic Recovery program to Congress, Reagan enumerated his principal objectives verbatim in the following excerpt:

> "...I have come to speak to you tonight about our economic recovery program and why I believe it's essential that the Congress approve this package, which I believe will lift the crushing burden of inflation off of our citizens and restore the vitality to our economy and our industrial machine...
>
> ...On behalf of the administration, let me say that we embrace and fully support that bipartisan substitute. It will achieve all the essential aims of controlling government spending, reducing the tax burden, building a national defense second to none, and stimulating economic growth and creating millions of new jobs...
>
> Let us cut through the fog for a moment. The answer to a government that's too big is to stop feeding its growth. Government spending has been growing faster than the economy itself. The massive national debt which we accumulated is the result of the government's high spending diet. Well, it's time to change the diet and to change it in the right way...
>
> ...A gigantic tax increase has been built into the system. We propose nothing more than a reduction of that increase. The people have a right to know that even

> with our plan they will be paying more in taxes, but not as much more as they will without it.
>
> ...Tonight, I renew my call for us to work as a team, to join in cooperation so that we find answers which will begin to solve all our economic problems and not just some of them. The economic recovery package that I've outlined to you over the past weeks is, I deeply believe, the only answer that we have left...
>
> ...Reducing the growth of spending, cutting marginal tax rates, providing relief from overregulation, and following a noninflationary and predictable monetary policy are interwoven measures which will ensure that we have addressed each of the severe dislocations which threaten our economic future. These policies will make our economy stronger, and the stronger economy will balance the budget which we're committed to do by 1984...
>
> When you allowed me to speak to you here in these chambers a little earlier, I told you that I wanted this program for economic recovery to be ours -- yours and mine. I think the bipartisan substitute bill has achieved that purpose. It moves us toward economic vitality, (Ronald Reagan Presidential Library Speeches, Address on the Program for Economic Recovery, Joint Session of Congress, 1).

Remarkably, even liberal Democrats found it diplomatically appeasing as an explicit "willingness to incorporate their own advantages into the bill illustrated effective utilization of special interests and sage public policy," (*Gould – The Modern American Presidency, 198*). Ultimately, compromise thrived. Accepted unanimously, President Reagan's unparalleled tax reform program managed to stifle inflation and facilitate occupational opportunities by adopting *supply-side economics.*

Supply side economic theory stipulates that tax cuts encourage "personal investment", which if implemented properly, fosters industrialization and economic hypertrophy, thus enhancing productivity, providing additional occupational opportunities necessary to generate sufficient revenue, and when combined with reduced spending, "balances the budget," thereby diminishing inflation (*DeGregorio – The Complete Book of U.S. Presidents 652*). Economists, impressed by the innovation, later labeled it *Reagonomics*. However, Reagan's Vice President and rival at the time, George H.W. Bush in a disparaging tone, criticized it as "Voodoo Economics" (*DeGregorio – The Complete Book of U.S. Presidents 652*).

Supply-Side "Reagonomics" maintained four fundamental principles: reduce government expenditure, diminish marginal tax rates on income, including, "labor and capital", minimize regulation, curtail inflation by, "controlling growth of money supply," (*Niskanen*, 1). Reagonomics, with its unregulated laissez faire capitalistic initiative, proved a monumental achievement to refurbish the pathetically phlegmatic American economy. Fiscal conservatism paved its progress.

Thus, through his practical, prudent understanding of frugality, minimizing superfluous expenditure, particularly welfare programs, while simultaneously stimulating occupational opportunities, in the private sector, Reagan introduced another remarkable presidential innovation. According to supply side theory, diminishing taxes for all groups, while simultaneously eradicating, "six million low income families from the tax income rolls," encouraged significant economic incentives, promoting labor, savings, and investment (*Sloan, The Reagan Effect…*, 7).

Consequently, due to his notable achievement, "the typical liberal member of Congress," today maintains a fiscal policy more conservative than, "Richard Nixon" involving numerous economic issues, including, tax policy (*Weisbrot*, 1). Thus, Reagan introduced an economic policy that irrevocably transformed the ideological perception of government leaders to produce a positive effect upon sanctioning subsequent initiatives, thereby ameliorating financial conditions for American taxpayers.

During this time, Reagan collaborated with his erudite chairman, William Joseph Casey, distinguished lawyer, to facilitate tax reform. Ultimately, Casey proved invaluably resourceful. A connoisseur of fiscal policy, he profoundly influenced Reagan's economic policy. Reagan summoned his formidable legal expertise to coordinate such programs including the Economic Recovery Tax Act. Casey, an incandescent intellectual, "tax attorney" and prominent political analyst for Reagan, proved indispensable to policy implementation (Columbia Encyclopedia, Sixth Edition, 1). Without Casey, the Economic Recovery Act and Reagonomics as an economic philosophy, cease to exist, if not for his unprecedented contributions, outlining effective strategies to revitalize America's economy and reduce unnecessary taxes.

Later, Reagan appointed Casey to serve as his CIA Direction, where he expanded executive power, government confidentiality, and clandestine activity. He represents one among numerous central figures connected to Iran Contra and its sequence of covert activities (D'Souza, 153). Thanks to his unsurpassed contributions, Reagan escaped criminal culpability, exonerated of all charges associated with Iran Contra. For now, consider the unprecedented economic contributions of William Casey as Chairman representing Reagan's campaign committee (Spartacus, Education, 1).

In July 1981, Reagan sanctioned the, Economic Recovery Tax Act. Serving as, "the largest tax reduction in U.S. history," it diminished personal income taxes by "25%", curtailed "capital gains" along with "estate taxes," and depreciated "business taxes," (*American National Biography Online, 7*). In 1982, ERTA offered a tax cut that exceeded, "$37 billion", attaining, "$267 billion," by 1986, culminating at an eventual revenue loss of, "$750 billion," (*Sloan, The Reagan Effect...*, 145). The 13% + inflation rate that once existed when Reagan assumed office, fell to, "below 2 percent in 1986 and sustained at around 4-5%," (*DeGregorio – The Complete Book of U.S. Presidents, 653*).

However, some adverse consequences temporarily accompanied this profound development. Apparently, the same high interest rates that moderated inflation, simultaneously compelled an already feeble economy into "severe recession", which, before collapsing in "November 1982", heightened apprehensions of "another depression," (*DeGregorio – The Complete Book of U.S. Presidents, 653*). While unemployment skyrocketed, "to 10.8%, its highest rate since the Great Depression, with bankruptcies and farm foreclosures reaching record levels," economic expansion eventually counterbalanced these effects, and unemployment gradually descended to "5.3%" (*DeGregorio – The Complete Book of U.S. Presidents*, 653).

Yet, Reagan never underestimated the tragic unemployment rates that unfortunately resulted as he verbatim asserts,

> "The economic crisis of the early 1980s brought hard times for Americans. I don't undervalue for a moment the suffering they experienced as we fought together to pull the nation out of its worst economic crisis in half a century. For those who lost their farms or businesses or saw their jobs vanish during the recession, life was as bleak as it was for Americans caught up in the economic upheavals of the Great Depression..." (Reagan, An American Life, 342).

Moreover, as Reagan further mentioned, the American people in general, though responding to him with varied reactions, remained receptive and acknowledged our national resilience, which one twenty seven year old mother of three at that time, astutely professed, "I think it's time...we as a country came off our high horses and got back to business of living with pride and independence," (*Reagan, Ronald*, "Reagan, An American Life", 343). Reagan recognized this general optimism expressed by Americans and channeled it to accomplish his lofty aspirations for the U.S. economy. Ultimately, his utilitarian sacrifice through ETRA in the long run proved significantly successful. Reagan retired from office establishing"20 million new jobs," with a whopping "118 million Americans achieving employment; the most ever in history," (*DeGregorio – The Complete Book of U.S. Presidents 653*).

To further accelerate economic growth, Reagan administered the U.S. Canadian Trade Pact of 1988 with Prime Minister Brian Mulroney in agreement, "to establish virtual free trade between both countries, abolishing taxes on goods and services progressively until 1999," (*DeGregorio – The Complete Book of U.S. Presidents*, 653). He ultimately succeeded in his agenda of, "creating a nation once again, vibrant, robust and alive," (*Morris – Dutch, A Memoir of Ronald Reagan*, 556). Hence, Reagan revitalized the previously depressed American economy, restoring its vitality.

Concerning domestic policy, Reagan challenged much of the liberal bureaucracy which sustained precedence since FDR's New Deal. For example, his administration sought to minimize "social welfare, alongside federal judicial involvement in promoting civil liberties; eliminate government regulation imposed on business, as mentioned earlier; and encouraged a conservative social ethic that emphasized religion within the public realm, which advocated pro-life principles regarding reproductive rights, and minimized drug use," (*American National Biography Online*, 7).

While Reagan endorsed some staunch anti-abortion measures, his overall position remained mostly moderate, not challenging the Roe v. Wade decision. America witnessed a notable conservative transition. Nancy Reagan contributed considerably to curtail drug abuse, collaborating with her husband in an anti-drug campaign known as "Just Say No" directing attention toward the youth of America (*D'Souza*, 221). President Reagan even targeted international support to deter drug sale and manufacture, especially cocaine, pursuing a vociferous anti-drug agenda (Reagan Library, The Reagan Presidency, 1).

Reagan most truly represented the common American. He revitalized American commitment to democratic freedom and nationalism. Patriotism centralized the theme of his conservative foundation, inculcating a true passion for America and its inexorable dedication to democracy. Reagan also believed in the multifarious, multicultural diversity defining democratic institutions. Unlike his predecessors, both liberal and conservative, Reagan seemed the most tolerant, showing no bigotry toward any groups. In fact, Reagan even remained responsible for commemorating Martin Luther King Jr.'s birthday, celebrating it as a national holiday (Hannity, 238). On Friday, January 14, 1983, Reagan recognized a, "reception" he dedicated to "honor memory of Martin Luther King Jr.", as expressed in his personal journal (Brinkley, Reagan, 125). Thus, this day holds profound historical significance, institutionalizing a standard subsequently practiced by Americans, honoring the unprecedented contributions of Martin Luther King Jr. to contemporary society.

In addition to inhibiting excessive federal infringement, Reagan micromanaged, "the regulations promulgated by federal agencies," (*Mc Donald – The American Presidency*, 343). Thus, in 1981 and 1985, he mandated, Executive Orders 12291 and 12498, as a means of assigning greater executive responsibility to agency administrators, "regarding the regulatory actions conducted within their agencies, which additionally included providing presidential oversight with assisting regulation," (*Mc Donald, The American Presidency*, 343).

This newly expanded delegation of power to federal agencies, assigning them executive constitutional powers, represents another conspicuously innovative achievement introduced by Ronald Reagan. Because it authorized extended presidential scrutiny, Ronald Reagan gradually gathered greater insight into the programs affecting his administrative policy. He exercised heightened political control and influence to regulate and implement certain programs that normally exceeded his physical capability without it. Therefore, the Executive Orders hold monumental historical value, representing a paradigmatic transition of executive policy in modern American history.

Reagan aspired to restore traditional federalism as intended by our constitutional founders. A fervent federalist, Reagan sought balanced limited government that supported separation of powers. Essentially, all three branches of government operate in separate spheres, performing solely their own respective responsibilities. Stringent constitutional restrictions on government authority apply as enumerated in the Articles of Federal power. According to Reagan, like our constitutional founders preceding him, our Legislative branch only constructs laws, Judiciaries, through executive nomination, remain solely responsible for interpreting it, while the President, as executive, in its jurisdiction exclusively implements such statutes established by these former branches. Reagan's contemporary conservatism remained consistent with those lofty democratic values established by our constitutional founders.

On Monday, July 19, 1982, Reagan announced in his newly publicized personal diary the priority to, "...address several thousand enthusiastic supporters of Constitutional Amendment requiring balanced budget...," which he sincerely believed complied with our founders' intent for balancing federal power and expenditure (Reagan, Brinkley, 93, "Reagan Diaries"). After all, our Constitutional framers condemned, "No taxation without representation," and sought independence due to the oppressive economic measures and general tyranny imposed by an authoritarian British monarch.

Hence, they established a sovereign democratic republic that sought political, social, and economic balance, one moderated by federal limitations enumerated in the Constitution. Understanding the totality of his circumstances, Reagan recognized that society necessitated political, economic, and social reform. Therefore, he sought to restore federalism by acquiring legislative sanction of the federal budget, and an auxiliary constitutional amendment which buttressed it. On August 4th of 82,

Reagan successfully managed to sanction a constitutional amendment that reorganized the federal budget, winning, "69-31" (Reagan, Brinkley, 96).

During his earlier political crusades as governor, Reagan proved a prolific writer, expressing the grandiloquent philosophies promulgated by our forefathers, "taking it on himself to define liberty," particularly, "our founders' intent," concerning constitutional interpretation (Noonan, 39, "*When Character Was King*"). The autonomous exchange of his prose flowed with succinct "smoothness" and simplicity. Later, Reagan eventually translated these lofty rationalizations into incandescent words of wisdom, when he later identified the Declaration of Independence and U.S. Constitution as, "covenants…made not only with ourselves but with all mankind," (D'Souza, 161, *How An Extraordinary Man Became an Extraordinary Leader*). Thus, most importantly, Reagan recognized the purpose of these monumental documents, as a social contract, to promote democratic equality and reciprocation among Americans. Its principles, as Reagan believed, facilitated the fundamental framework and foundation of democratic freedom.

Moreover, like Jefferson, Madison, Hamilton, Jay, and Adams, Reagan favored a strong central government, that authorized separate equal powers for states, to operate within their own jurisdiction. Reagan championed federalism. Encouraging development within the private sector, Reagan pursued federalism, transferring some federal government responsibilities to states (Reagan Library, The Reagan Presidency, 1). He completely consolidated and reorganized the separation of powers to suit transitioning trends. However, unlike traditional federalism, Reagan renovated this originalist constitutional concept to correspond with contemporary standards, another profound innovation of the Reagan presidency.

New federalism models seek to, "reverse centralizing tendencies in American government," thereby restoring separate, "balance of power between nations and states," as intended by our constitutional framers

(Dye, Thomas, 13). Hence, Reagan introduced the paradigm of *new federalism*, which sought to increase, "power and program authority for states plus localities," (Bowman, Kearney, *State and Local Government*, 38). For example, under Reagan's new federalism initiative, states individually regulated their own statutes regarding "welfare and food stamps," (Palmer, Sawhill, 12).

While many political scientists accord Richard Nixon with this innovation, only Reagan's brand of "new federalism" succeeded to heighten state authority, and restore balanced, separate powers as intended by our constitutional framers. Essentially, Reagan elaborated upon such policies introduced by Nixon, integrating his own uniquely innovative administrative style, "broadening even further," as new federalism adapted to the "legitimate scope" which defines, "the public sector," (Conlan, 5). Thus, through new federalism, Reagan believed autonomous communities possess the self-sovereign capability to resolve moral conflicts, "governing themselves at a local level (*D'Souza*, 263). Hence, President Ronald W. Reagan revolutionized the conventional American constitutional concept of federalism, tailoring its originalist philosophy to more suitably accommodate contemporary challenges.

This pattern of administering greater power to states not only ameliorated intergovernmental interaction, but minimized federal bureaucracy as Reagan intended. President Reagan managed to incorporate new federalism in the following ways. First, he forced states to assume greater responsibility regarding state issues, or any legal controversies not presenting a federal challenge. Reagan achieved congressional approval to consolidate "57 categorical grants into nine blocks," and thereby obliterate an additional, "60 categorical grants," (Bowman, Kearney, *State and Local Government*, 38).

For political expedience, Reagan delegated greater authority to states, yet compromised block grants, decreasing its funds by almost "25%" from its previous allocation for the separate categorical grants (Conlan,

"*Federalism and Competing Values*..., 29-47). Hence, Reagan proposed that the federal government eliminate, "most highway programs," while terminating, "federal gasoline taxes" supporting them (Edwards, Federalism and Separation of Powers, 4). Hence, Reagan restored the sound fiscal policy intended by our constitutional founders through his own innovative modern brand of federalism.

When Ronald Reagan assumed the presidency, "checking court tendencies ranked high on his agenda," (*Mc Donald, The American Presidency*, 304). He executed this judicial initiative through his punctilious appointment of federal judges, "scrupulously screening prospective nominees for ability, integrity and most importantly judicial philosophy," unlike other Presidents before Reagan who self-centeredly, "appointed cronies or minorities, seeking to enhance their presidential reputation," (*Mc Donald – The American Presidency*, 304). His avaricious predecessors sought only to accommodate their own partisan propagandist platforms, provincial lobbyist agendas, and personal interests, exploiting their pernicious initiatives at the virulent expense of society.

While others employed demagoguery and demoralized American democracy, Reagan remained consummately committed to his independent conservative values, never nominating a judge for reasons concerning political prestige. Reagan only cared about the utilitarian welfare of America. However, as Reagan himself professed, that politics overall, specifically the Democratic Party, "...In 1984...became a conglomeration of blocs and special-interest groups, each with narrow special agendas directed at grabbing more of the national wealth for their own interests," (*Reagan, Ronald*, "Reagan, An American Life", 325).

Judicial appointment ranks among the most significant aspects of executive power, because it determines national policy for subsequent years. For Reagan, it signified the restoration of conservative libertarian constitutional values to American society. Regarding judicial philosophy, Reagan nominated strict constructionist judges, restoring federalism to constitutional interpretation. His nominations comprised four Supreme Court appointments, including former Chief Justice William Rehnquist, in addition to associate justices Sandra Day O' Conor, Antonin Scalia, and Anthony Kennedy (*American National Biography*, 13). On July 7, 1981, Sandra Day O' Connor became, "the first woman" in American history to serve on the nation's highest court (CNN Interactive, Video Almanac, 1). Antonin Scalia emerged to become the Supreme Court's, "principal defender of presidential power against Congressional or Judicial encroachment," (*DeGregorio – The Complete Book of U.S. Presidents 658*). Since Supreme Court Judges serve lifetime tenure, Reagan's judicial appointments exercise profound permanent impact on constitutional interpretation, signaling a general conservative transition for years to follow.

Ronald Reagan castigated the cruel nature of partisan politics in a manner analogous to how George Washington criticized partisanship during his time. In Washington's time, inflammatory rivalries fomented hostility between the Federalists and Jeffersonian Republicans. Much like Washington, Reagan found it sophomoric. Today, Reagan witnessed the same rhetoric between Republicans and Democrats. However, the founders never anticipated, nor conceived this intense level of scathing, acrimonious dispute in contemporary America. Yet, Reagan overcame this frivolous partisan nonsense, concentrating upon the more mature, practical matters affecting America.

Since his inauguration, Ronald Reagan restored moral providence to its national consciousness in American society. A vehement patriotic American himself, Reagan understood in totality, the value of national presence. Yet, like our constitutional founders, enlightenment philosophers such as John Locke, including natural law advocates who preceded them, particularly St. Thomas Aquinas, Reagan also recognized a moral duty to acknowledge, with gratitude, the gift of such freedom bestowed by God. For example, on March 19, 1981, Reagan acknowledged a "National Day of Prayer" in Proclamation 4826, verbatim promulgating that,

> "...In God We Trust" -- was not chosen lightly. It reflects a basic recognition that there is a divine authority in the universe to which this Nation owes homage... Throughout our history Americans have put their faith in God and no one can doubt that we have been blessed for it. The earliest settlers of this land came in search of religious freedom. Landing on a desolate shoreline, they established a spiritual foundation that has served us ever since...It was the hard work of our people, the freedom they enjoyed and their faith in God that built this country and made it the envy of the world... While never willing to bow to a tyrant, our forefathers were always willing to get to their knees before God. When catastrophe threatened, they turned to God for deliverance. When the harvest was bountiful the first thought was thanksgiving to God... Now, Therefore, I, Ronald Reagan, President of the United States of America, do hereby proclaim Thursday, May 7, 1981, National Day of Prayer. On that day I ask all who believe to join with me in giving thanks to Almighty God for the blessings He has bestowed on this land and the protection He affords us as a people. Let us as a Nation join together before God, fully aware of the trials that lie ahead and the need, yes, the necessity, for divine guidance. With unshakeable faith in God and the liberty which is heritage, we as a free Nation will surely survive and prosper... In Witness Whereof, I have hereunto set my hand this nineteenth day of March, in year of our Lord nineteen hundred and eighty-one, and of the Independence of the United States of America the two hundred and fifth. Ronald Reagan," (Reagan Library, 1, Proclamation 4826).

Reagan's pronouncement of God, maintained a uniquely secular, spiritual element. It served solely to trigger national response and inspire faith in the American people. Ironically, Reagan's religious fervor and national sentiment reflect a personal spiritual nature not cemented in the context of any particular religion. After all, Reagan seldom attended church services during his presidency, perhaps consumed with tremendous responsibilities, serving the nation, which asserted precedence (*DeGregorio – The Complete Book of U.S. Presidents, 637*). Still, Reagan sustained irrevocable faith in God. As Ron Jr. revealed at Reagan's funeral in 2004,

> "Dad was also a deeply, unabashedly religious man. But he never made the fatal mistake of so many politicians of wearing his faith in his sleeve to gain political advantage," (*Coulter*, "How to Talk to a Liberal (If You Must)").

Rather, Reagan remained inexorably true to his venerable virtue, unlike others who engaged in demagoguery and utilized religion for subversive purposes.

Reagan sought to preserve the strong Judeo-Christian tradition, an indispensable element of our constitutional foundation. Yet, this glorious Day of Prayer only reinforces nationalism, moral servitude, and democratic values, in a consistent constitutional manner that avoids indoctrinating any particular religious establishment. Hence, he restored moral providence and patriotic presence to American society. While, "not a conventionally religious man," as D'Souza succinctly stipulates, he possessed, "providential understanding of destiny," the intuitive prudence, prescience, sagacity, and vision to effect history (*D'Souza*, 28).

With unadulterated optimism, an incessant positive demeanor, the president never abandoned his faith. Such faith provided unsurpassed strength. He always stood steadfast in the face of adversity. Reagan encountered tremendous tribulations. Yet, no challenge ever appeared insurmountable. Why? He understood, better than his contemporary predecessors, the profound significance of personal faith. It gave him a sense of purpose and direction. Reagan's confidence, conviction, countenance and character, remained unassailable. Consequently, his formidable foundation of faith proved an invaluable ideological commitment that facilitated subsequent American success. Ultimately, Reagan translated his inexorable moral faith into action, because he truly believed in the inevitability of, "good prevailing over evil," (*D'Souza*, 28).

Reagan also invigorated presidential authority domestically, managing an unwarranted strike imposed by PATCO, the Professional Air Traffic Controllers Organization. Reagan aggressively confronted the arrogant and avaricious labor organization evoking, "a sense of public drama," (Gould, 198). Ironically, PATCO represented, "one of the few unions that supported his candidacy," (D'Souza, 230). Recognizing their rather reasonable complaint, President Reagan initially promised to compensate strikers, offering an, "11%" pay raise, but because the belligerent ungrateful union unjustifiably demanded "100%" increase, intervention proved imperative (Noonan, 222). Pure unadulterated 'Boulwarism' in action Reagan assumed an aggressive position to deter the intransigent labor union, who refused his command. In a forceful ultimatum, Reagan exhorted their return to work within "48 hours" (Evans, 204). Reagan followed his words and fired the insubordinate unionists who refused to return.

By establishing his powerful authoritative presence, Reagan's stature increased because the nation utterly appreciated a chief executive "who supervised unwaveringly, unlike his incompetent liberal predecessor Jimmy Carter on numerous occasions," (Gould, 198). Carter usually vacillated when confronted with similar challenge. He lacked the indispensable, "political wisdom" and volitional capability to efficiently adjudicate, or render, "political judgments about policy decisions," (Sloan, John, 41). What a refreshing change! Through painstaking punctilious precision, stringently regulating PATCO, meticulously monitoring its program to ensure public safety, Reagan once again exhibited formidable leadership qualities as president. Hence, through his inexorably rigorous, resolute administrative demeanor, Reagan restored power, presence, and prestige to the presidency, proving himself a preeminent political leader. He exuded superior statesmanship. Likewise, Reagan retained this same tough-minded tenacity and robust resolution regarding foreign policy, as in his domestic interactions. He never once surrendered in submission nor acquiesced to the dictates of others.

Early 21st Century international terrorism, evolving prematurely in its preliminary phase under Reagan, references another revolutionary paradigm regarding the modern presidency. Consequently, such technological advancement catalyzed societal transformations, which simultaneously encouraged terrorism, cultivating an atmosphere most conducive to its proliferation. Disparity between Western and Middle Eastern culture fomented in widespread terror. Islamic extremists, barbarous Jihadist organizations who despised American values, began unleashing their belligerent contempt for the U.S and its Judeo-Christian founded democratic lifestyle.

These psychotic fundamentalists, synonymous with terrorism, consumed by their bigotry, attempt to justify mass murder, violence, and genocide in the name of God, or Allah. Hence, in recent years, Middle Eastern terrorism subsequently became the new nefarious nemesis pervading American policy. Strangely, such latent sentiments, which manifested and began to materialize, initiated in its preliminary phase during the Reagan presidency. Nonetheless, notwithstanding these dramatic institutional and societal transformations sweeping over society, Reagan persevered, pursuing a rigorously aggressive foreign policy, to ravage the ruthless enemy.

As technological innovation accelerated, irrevocably altering the global landscape, terrorists discovered increasingly insidious methods to infiltrate attack. Unfortunately, *globalization*, the process by which political, social, and cultural institutions become internationally interdependent, simplifies transportation, thus fostering dissemination of terrorism. With globalization expanding and ultimately reaching the forefront of technological development, terrorism became a fundamental theme for 21st Century international policy. Essentially, the increased prevalence of terrorism targeting America proved an unparalleled challenge for Reagan and subsequent presidents.

Still, Reagan never acquiesced to adversity. He proceeded without trepidation. From the beginning, Reagan demanded, "swift retribution against international terrorism," (*DeGregorio – The Complete Book of U.S. Presidents 654*). Again, despite relentless resistance, the U.S. in no manner managed to prevent or exempt itself from its inexorable susceptibility toward terrorism. As its precursor, this period inevitably foreshadows the present situation surrounding post 9/11/2001 America. Inversely analogous to the concluding U.S.-Soviet Cold War communism era, which Reagan conquered, America today commences a different international cultural war, its confrontation with terrorism, or as contemporarily known, "The War Against Terror". Yet, modern terrorism emerged in its infancy during Reagan's presidency.

Reagan became president during an era characterized by heightened, regional crisis circulating throughout the Middle East. Along with Soviet imperialistic occupation of Afghanistan and the belligerent Iranian regime, Iraq attacked Iran, attempting to overthrow Ayatollah Khomeini, a virulent terrorist (Smith, Charles, 365). Hence, by 1982, the U.S. pursued a policy of military intervention to mediate acrimonious dispute between Israelis and Palestinians. Again Reagan sought to resolve the recalcitrant dispute primarily between two diametrically opposed reactionary regimes, Israel and Egypt. Moreover, Reagan aspired to establish compromise between the two principal nefarious nemeses, Israelis and Palestinians, in Middle Eastern geopolitics. As usual, Reagan pursued a foreign policy strategy of political realism, principally idealistic in its ultimate aspirations, securing peace for the area.

In April 1983, Iranian terrorists infiltrated, "an explosion at the U.S. embassy in Beirut which killed 16 Americans and dozens of other troops," (*Gould – The Modern American Presidency, 200*). Reagan stood steadfast. America endorsed Israel's objective to eradicate PLO influence from peace negotiations. However, the U.S. became disgusted with Israel's perfunctory disregard toward civilian lives. Its imperialist international position not only insulted American foreign policy, but instigated suspicion.

President Reagan assumed a preemptive strategy against Israel. Intervention remained the only solution. Recognizing its political usurpation, Reagan introduced the Reagan Plan, which revitalized Camp David Accords, thwarting Israeli claims to settlements extending along the West Bank, refusing Israeli possession and sovereignty of any area, including Gaza (Smith, 380). Still, Reagan repudiated establishment of an autonomous Palestinian state. He objected on the grounds that Resolution 242, promulgated in 1967, which sought equal coexistence between Israelis and Palestinians, withdrawal of occupied territories, applied inclusively to both groups.

Many modern historians consider such oscillation in foreign policy between defending Israelis yet Palestinians naturally contradictory. Such an observation neglects the forceful diplomatic dexterity employed by Reagan to carefully counteract crisis and simultaneously appease both groups, endorsing collective interests, thereby exploiting U.S. policy toward American advantage. Both Reagan and his Secretary of State George Shultz empathized with both groups recognizing, "the legitimate needs and problems of Palestinians," necessitated resolution "urgently" in its entirety (Spiegel, Steven, 419). However, Reagan's bold attempt obviously failed because it neglected, never intended to consider the PLO extremists. Reagan deemed this group intransigent and ideologically impenetrable, thereby overlooking their radical recalcitrant concerns.

Again, modern terrorism emerged and became rampant throughout the Middle East. For example, the 1982 stationing of U.S. Marines in Lebanon, attempting to resolve Middle Eastern tension, triggered an October 1983 terrorist bombing that killed 241 barricaded troops (*Gould – The Modern American Presidency, 200*). Reagan substantiated that stationing the marines in Lebanon proved, "central to U.S. credibility on a global scale," flexing its military muscle against Communism, as a preventative measure, securing Lebanon from becoming subsumed by Soviet control (Smith, Charles, 384).

By conducting this military assault, "Iranian radicals drove trucks loaded with explosives into the U.S. Marine headquarters at Beirut airport, which annihilated a French compound nearby, additionally killing another 50 located there," (*DeGregorio – The Complete Book of U.S. Presidents 654*). When civil war resurged nearly 4 months later between, "Lebanese Moslems and Christians," Reagan evacuated Marines to ships offshore the Mediterranean. (*DeGregorio – The Complete Book of U.S. Presidents 654*). These attacks signify the "first major incidences of terrorism directed against the U.S., and after recognizing America's vulnerability, Muslim Fundamentalists, who sincerely hate American hegemony, terrorism thus proved a persisting problem," (*Gould – The Modern American Presidency, 200*).

Around June 1985, conflict resumed as an entourage of, "Shiite Moslem extremists hijacked a TWA jetliner flight heading to Rome from Athens, with 153 passengers aboard, including 104 Americans," (*DeGregorio – The Complete Book of U.S. Presidents 653*). This resulted in the assassination of one U.S. Navy diver. While they surprisingly released all remaining hostages, this however, occurred only after finally, "winning freedom for the Shiite prisoners held hostage in Israel," (*DeGregorio – The Complete Book of U.S. Presidents 653*).

Then in October 1985, Palestinian Liberation Front (PLF) members hijacked the *Achille Lauro*, an Italian ship traveling to Egypt, and murdered one elderly, paralyzed American. They thereafter threw him, Leon Linghoffer, a "helpless wheelchair-bound" into the Mediterranean Sea (Noonan, 267). Consequently, the U.S. retaliated. Upon their surrender, after Egyptian authorities guaranteed safe departure from Egypt, audacious U.S. Navy F-14 fighters arrived and bravely performed their own hijacking, exhorting the Egyptian plane to land in Sicily, where Italian authorities then incarcerated PLO members (*DeGregorio – The Complete Book of U.S. Presidents 653*). Two months later, another isolated incident followed when, "Palestinian terrorists opened fire in the Rome and Vienna Airport terminals, killing 20, including an 11year old girl plus 4 other Americans," (*DeGregorio – The Complete Book of U.S. Presidents 653*). In April 1986, a West Berlin Discotheque exploded, killing one American serviceman and additionally injuring 60 other Americans. In retaliation, "U.S. F-111 fighter planes bombed Tripoli, annihilating Muammar Qaddafi's home, military targets, civilian homes and the French embassy," (*DeGregorio – The Complete Book of U.S. Presidents 653*).

Again, as time progressed proportionately with technological advancement, terrorists increasingly discovered more insidious methods to perpetrate attack. For instance, On Dec. 21, 1988, a Pan Am passenger jet exploded over Lockerbie, Scotland, slaughtering all "259 aboard" and "11" of its the ground. Police later discovered the concealed bomb attached to an audiocassette player, (PBS – The American Experience Timeline, 5). The Reagan administration directly associated five nations, "Iran, Libya, North Korea, Cuba, and Nicaragua – with international terrorism," (*DeGregorio – The Complete Book of U.S. Presidents 653*). Reagan isolated Libyan Muammar Qaddafi, "as the world's principal terrorist," (*DeGregorio – The Complete Book of U.S. Presidents 653*). After recognizing the source, he immediately tackled it.

In May 1981, the Reagan administration "expelled all Libyan diplomats, terminating their mission assigned at Washington," upon discovering charges of attempted murder directed against Libyan dissidents who resided in the U.S (*DeGregorio – The Complete Book of U.S. Presidents, 653*). Both in 1981 and 89 U.S. Navy Jets intercepted Libyan fighter planes, which posed a perceptible danger along the Libyan coast. Despite these seemingly marginal, "minor military operations," they favorably projected, "the impression of a [powerful] President prepared to use force," in defending American interests (Mandelbaum, 133). In January 1986, Reagan prohibited all international activities with Libya, exhorted complete American departure from the country to preserve public safety, and threatened military intervention against Libya if it continued to endorse terrorism (*DeGregorio – The Complete Book of U.S. Presidents, 653*). Though many countries condemned the 1986 West Berlin Discotheque retaliation, as a supposed act of terrorism within itself Reagan persisted without hesitation.

The Reagan administration adopted a propaganda campaign that deliberately encouraged dissent within Libya, and professed imminent attack. Of course, after posting fabricated stories, featuring decorated distortions, "in the *Wall Street Journal* among other reputable newspapers, such media exposure exploded with inflammatory leftist criticism. Furthermore, Reagan also intimated the probability of targeting Libya with additional assault, in attempt to eradicate what America perceived a potentially threatening, chemical warfare plant (*DeGregorio – The Complete Book of U.S. Presidents, 653*).

The invasion of Grenada in 1983 also exhibited striking success. On October 1983, U.S. forces invaded West Indies Island, Grenada, "the smallest Western Hemisphere nation", to rescue hundreds of Americans threatened by a leftist military regime," (*DeGregorio – The Complete Book of U.S. Presidents, 657*). After dismantling the communist government, rescuing American medical students, this event signified notable triumph, inevitably foreshadowing re-election for Reagan. Americans overwhelmingly approved of the invasion. The Reagan administration exercised its military muscle, dispatching "5,000" U.S. troops, and ultimately, prevailed (PBS – The American Experience Timeline, 4). Deterring a relatively feeble adversary, "the achievement appeared more gratifying from a public relations perspective," (*Gould*, 201). The U.S. affirmed its formidable military prowess, which stimulated a sense of public security, positive sentiment, and awareness among Americans. Cognizant citizens praised the victory. Consequently, it proved a win-win situation. The inexpensive conflict, "bolstered presidential prestige at minimal expense to American interest, and Ronald Reagan," (*Gould*, 201).

Other aspects of foreign policy proved slightly less than successful for the Reagan administration. The modern presidency began to reveal its constitutional limitations. Circumstances like the 1985 *Iran Contra Affair* elucidate such limitations. Nevertheless, Reagan overcame presidential blunder, whereby he eventually succeeded in securing the hostages, escaping fallacious indictments, and through complete convalescence, revived his popularity, which skyrocketed to an unparalleled "86 percent among young Americans, eight days after renewing contra aid," (*Morris – Dutch, A Memoir of Ronald Reagan*, 577). Still, the Iran Contra scandal proved a critical setback of drastic proportions for Reagan.

In Iran, problems relentlessly persisted with government sequestration of Americans. Throughout the 1980s, Hezbollah, a pro-Iranian terrorist organization, captured and sadistically tortured American hostages (Noonan, 265). The secretive sale of arms to Iran emanated with Israel (Schlesinger, 252-53). Government intelligence conducted clandestine operations to secure American hostages sequestered by Iranian terrorists under the direct supervision of CIA Director William Casey. Casey arranged the delivery of weapons to Iran (Spartacus, 1). However, to this day, Casey's actual association with Iran Contra remains elusive and mysterious, since he suffered a severe stroke shortly after the scandal became public, and died one year thereafter, in 1987, before any opportunity of ever disclosing any details of his involvement (Columbia Encyclopedia, Sixth Edition, 1). Nevertheless, the "Iran-Contra Final Report" concluded that Casey, "played a role…in [organizing] the covert networks to supply contras…and promoting secret arms sales to Iran…," (FAS, "Iran-Contra Report", 1).

The President responded diplomatically, even resorting to desperate measures. He negotiated a compromise with Iran, "agreeing to sell them arms surreptitiously, in exchange for the release of American hostages," (*DeGregorio – The Complete Book of U.S. Presidents*, 655). Exasperated by his inability to rescue Americans, Reagan vociferously declared, "I don't care if I have to go to Leavenworth; I want the hostages out," (*DeGregorio*

– *The Complete Book of U.S. Presidents*, 655). Even so, the kidnapping of Americans unabatedly continued. Unfortunately, his compassionate attempt backfired. Circumstances culminated in controversy when a Lebanese periodical exposed the entire weapon deal.

The situation grew so abominably disarrayed that thoughts of, "*impeachment* reverberated throughout Capitol Hill," (*Morris – Dutch, A Memoir of Ronald Reagan*, 616). Meanwhile, Reagan utterly oblivious as to what occurred possessed no, "prior knowledge of the Iran-Contra connection," (*Neustadt – Presidential Power and the Modern Presidents, 283*). The evidence overwhelmingly indicates that he knew nothing about it. Reagan admitted in his personal diary that neither Oliver North nor John Poindexter informed him of the scandal. On November 24, 1986, Ronald Reagan privately confessed in the diary,

> "On one of the arms shipments the Iranians paid Israel a higher purchase price than we were getting… Then our North giving the contras money without an authorization by Congress. North didn't tell me anything about this. Worst of all John Poindexter found out about it & didn't tell me. This may call for resignations." (Brinkley, Reagan, 453).

This message substantially suggests the scandal occurred without his consent, exonerating him of culpability. The illicit weapons deal occurred unbeknownst to him. Thus, Reagan remained innocent. He only intended to save the seven American citizens held hostage by reactionary Islamic militias associated with Iran. Instead, North engaged in an unlawful covert operation that inadvertently framed the President.

Private middlemen who manufactured these armaments, exorbitantly overcharged Iran, dispatching approximately "one-fourth" of all its profits to the contras, "anti-Sandinistas fighting in Nicaragua" (*DeGregorio – The Complete Book of U.S. Presidents, 655*). The contras, counterrevolutionaries, or reactionaries, sought to dismantle an oppressive communist regime, and establish their national sovereignty. As mentioned earlier, the President pledged never to sanction any agreements with terrorists. Reagan denied trading arms for hostages, insisting that he instead, "exchanged to renew ties with Iranian moderates," (*DeGregorio – The Complete Book of U.S. Presidents, 655*).

Inundated with seemingly contrary evidence, Reagan conceded that the U.S. projected the appearance of engaging directly in "an arms–for –hostages swap". President Reagan appointed former Texas Senator, "John Tower to investigate the matter," (*DeGregorio – The Complete Book of U.S. Presidents*, 655). After several agonizing televised hearings, Security Adviser John Poindexter confessed his sanctioning of contra profit diversions without presidential consent, because he wanted to provide 'plausible deniability' in any case it became exposed (*DeGregorio – The Complete Book of U.S. Presidents*, 655). Poindexter additionally "destroyed the document" authorized by Reagan to avoid any possibility of causing him "political embarrassment," (*DeGregorio – The Complete Book of U.S. Presidents*, 655-6).

The plot coagulated when Colonel Oliver North publicly admitted that he fabricated and exterminated documents to clandestinely conceal information concerning administrative involvement in contra aid, but claimed that, "his superiors supposedly authorized every action, whom he thoroughly informed," (*DeGregorio – The Complete Book of U.S. Presidents*, 656). All along, North sold weapons to the contras, an overt breach of military conduct. He committed a felony. Federal law forbade any sale, manufacture, or lucrative exchange of arms to terrorists, no matter the circumstances. It prohibited any such profit diversion. Bottom line, regardless of the situation, laws remain unconditional unless authorized by Congress. Thus, without receiving legislative sanctioning, Oliver North violated federal law.

By receiving consent from high ranking personnel, North thought nothing wrong of it. To avoid any denied authority for utilization of funds, the men collected private money, which when construed, "not only meant private citizens, but also other governments," (*Neustadt – Presidential Power and the Modern Presidents*, 284). Accordingly, both men, including National Security Advisor Robert Mc Farlane , "conspired to privatizing contra aid by soliciting funds from friendly foreign governments, like Brunei, and affluent American conservatives such as Adolph Coors in supporting the guerrillas," (*American National Biography*, 12).

However, this scandal took a bizarre turn for the worst. The following events reference an intricate clandestine conspiracy characterized by chicanery, deception, plausible lies and untruths. North conceived what he considered a "neat idea: overcharging Iranians for American weapons, and using its profits to support Nicaraguan contras," (*American National Biography Online*, 12). Finally, "a 690-page report obtained by the committee confirmed Reagan's innocence, as he knew nothing about these illicit contra diversions, but blamed Reagan's laissez faire management style," (*DeGregorio – The Complete Book of U.S. Presidents*, 656). Walking away from mistaken indictments, Reagan appointed special prosecutor, Lawrence Walsh in March 1988, who "secured indictments for conspiracy, fraud, and theft of government funds," (*DeGregorio – The Complete Book of U.S. Presidents*, 656).

Though Reagan successfully survived *The Iran Contra Affair*, it most definitely demonstrates the dubious political and psychological challenges facing modern presidents, concerning executive limitations during their second terms. After all, 8 years as President of the United States proves an arduous process, imposing severe burden upon anyone who sustains such an extended tenure. However, to a certain extent, this incident diminished Reagan's public reputation, "reducing his great accomplishments," even if it inflicted marginal damage (Schlesinger, 259). Presidents become inexorably susceptible to limitations if they, "serve during a period that stimulates responsiveness in Congress toward perceived misconduct witnessed by recent, preceding presidents, exemplify illicit conduct, evade established channels of democratic accountability, and/or rely upon people who lack political competence," (*Malcolm Shaw – The Modern Presidency,304*). In addition, vulnerability to limitation also applies if, "certain aspects of foreign policy depict indefensibility," (*Malcolm Shaw – The Modern Presidency, 304*).

Evidently, Reagan corresponds to most, if not all of these categories. For example, with Nixon's Watergate scandal still reminiscent, congressional leaders, "during their joint investigation of the events wrote a section referring to 'Iran-gate'," which evoked numerous responses, questioning how much Reagan actually knew (*Malcolm Shaw – The Modern Presidency, 304*). As mentioned earlier, the affair violated Federal law on numerous accounts, and reflected poorly on Reagan. After all, the legal definition of negligence expects individuals, particularly individuals in esteemed executive positions, to possess knowledge and awareness regarding certain activities. If unlawful activities occur under the oversight of a corporation, complicity typically applies, holding executives vicariously liable for resulting actions. Both Federal and State law considers executives as primarily responsible for the administrative management of their corporation, and thereby, requires their awareness regarding employee activity. This identical aforementioned principle applies analogously to public office, politicians, and executive management.

Yet, one must consider the entire circumstances. The profit diversion proved imperative, a venerable sacrifice to protect American lives. Frankly, Oliver North among others acted heroically to preserve the lives of his fellow Americans. Military law, through executive power, guarantees extra-constitutional power during circumstances related to war. Hence, our government relinquishes certain fundamental constitutional powers to preserve the general welfare of Americans. Yet, by preserving the general welfare, in this case, rescuing American hostages, these men uphold our constitutional values. The U.S. Constitutional Preamble reflects this principle. As promulgated by Article I, Section 8, which incorporates the General Welfare Clause, specifically enumerates government power to accommodate, "the general welfare" of Americans, a "duty" which holds consistent, "throughout the U.S.," (Ducat, Craig, D3). Additionally, the Constitutional 'Supremacy Clause', Article VI, Section 2 acknowledges our U.S. Constitution as "the Supreme Law of the land," with all other statutes inferior and subordinate in jurisdiction to its command (Ducat, Craig, D7). Hence, since our U.S. Constitution, empowered superior authority, serves the utilitarian welfare of its citizens, America possesses a legal duty to protect collective liberties. We defend the collective liberties by rescuing our endangered American hostages. Therefore, the attempt to save hostages proved not only worthy, but a necessary cause. The "Necessary and Proper Clause" promulgated by Article I, Section 18, reinforces this indispensable duty to our threatened hostages.

However, the entire staff failed to provide President Reagan fair notice, and conducted these unlawful diversions in such a secretive manner that casts suspicion. Again, the clandestine confidential nature of this operation, covertly conducted, causes reasonable doubt. They pursued an illegal act without executive consent, failing to inform the president beforehand of their objective and report any underground conspiratorial activities. If Reagan instead knew about it, and administered approval to engage in the profit diversions, with Congressional consent, then circumstances change. Rather, he may not even need legislative sanction.

The U.S. Constitution accords additional presidential power during wartime, not permitted under ordinary circumstances. Obviously, a lingering hostage crisis constitutes extraordinary circumstances. Consider Article II, Sec. 2 which guarantees special powers to execute the laws as "Commander in Chief of the Army…Navy…and [state] militias…," (Ducat, Craig, D5). Various presidents throughout U.S. history interpret this clause to temporarily suspend certain constitutional liberties for the general welfare during wartime. During an extremely vulnerable, tempestuous period in American history, threatened by war, 2nd U.S. President, John Adams instituted the Alien and Sedition Acts, which prohibited pernicious infiltration of immigrants, and any subversive conduct deemed dangerous toward American interests. President Woodrow

Wilson resurrected this same Alien and Seditions acts measure during World War I, for similar reasons. In the Civil War, a period characterized by civil rebellion, President Abraham Lincoln temporarily suspended Habeas Corpus, denying a fundamental right of court appearance, without congressional approval. Hence, given such imminent threat, with Americans held hostage, the Constitution empowers Reagan an executive duty to secure them as deemed necessary and proper.

Moreover, even if Reagan knew the illicit acts committed by his staff, the crimes still surpass presidential scope. After all, the president, like any executive, delegates partial responsibility to his inferiors, who scrupulously scrutinize employee activities. A balanced separation of powers, which reflects American federalism, applies even within the three governmental subdivisions. The President appoints a staff, assigning specialized responsibilities to his closest advisors, removing such burdens which supersede administrative control. Thus, these individuals maintain a fiduciary trust and obligation to fulfill their task as expected of them.

Still, recent public records corroborate that Reagan never participated or associated in any way with the scandal which occurred. The whole scandal went completely unnoticed. Whether or not Reagan actually conspired in the scandal, his presidential position in no manner exonerates him from potential criminal liabilities incurred as a result of complicit activities committed by others. Presidential scope of influence requires that he develop utter awareness involving the unlawful underground activities resulting from conspirators within his own administration. Such scope entails knowledge concerning the following activities; "failure to notify Congress of covert U.S. operations, tampering with and destroying official documents, and illegally assisting the contras," (DeGregorio, 656).

Hence, presidential negligence still applies. Reagan's presidential duty prescribes a knowledge and cognizance of staff activities. Reagan lacked this indispensable legal requirement. Transferrable intent perhaps applies through vicarious liability, transporting intent under the scope of executive authority. Unquestionably, the incompetent staff surrounding Reagan also exacerbated his presidential restrictions. Reagan promoted former Secretary of the Treasury, Donald Regan to White House Chief of Staff. An irresponsible official, Donald Regan and his contributory negligence, as principle supervisor of inside executive operations, condoned such clandestine activities, allowing them to go unnoticed.

As aforementioned, Reagan felt naturally compelled to rescue the American hostages by whatever means necessary. To him, rescuing the hostages represented a moral obligation. With willingness to commit the ultimate sacrifice for those hostages, Reagan considered them as one of his children. He actually compared the hostages to his own children. The following analogy shows Reagan's sincere highest regard for human life. He follows the consummate compassion, benevolence, and altruistic sentiments emanating his soul to render a very challenging crucial decision. To Reagan, human life meant the highest sacrifice. Nothing compares to the generosity of this man, how he truly values human life. Reagan follows utilitarianism as a moral philosophy to rescue the hostages. Indeed, 'the end justifies the means' as 19th Century Utilitarian philosopher John Stuart Mill proposed, sacrificing to preserve human life and protect against violations of individual liberty. Reagan remained willing by whatever means necessary, regardless of consequences, to secure the hostages, because he most truly valued human life. As Reagan verbatim explained in an argument directed to Secretary of State George Schultz,

> "'Look I said, we all agree we can't pay ransom to the Hizballah to get the hostages. But we are not dealing with the Hizballah, we are not doing a thing for them. We are trying to help some people who are looking forward to becoming the next government of Iran, and they are getting the weapons in return…to free our hostages. It's the same as if one of my children was kidnapped and there was a demand for ransom; sure, I don't believe in ransom because it leads to more kidnapping. But if I find out there's somebody who has access to the kidnapper

> and can get my child back without doing anything for the kidnapper, I'd sure do that. And it would be perfectly fitting for me to reward that individual if he got my child back. That's not paying ransom to the kidnappers,' " (Noonan, 268).

A truly venerable, virtuous individual, Reagan believed in the prevalence of justice. However, to accomplish this end, he transcended his own presidential power authorized by the Constitution. By manipulating, "those aspects of the Constitution which interfered with his foreign policy agendas," he endured some troubling consequences (DeGregorio, 656). However, from a different perspective, Reagan exercised his executive Constitutional duty, by attempting to rescue those hostages, securing their lives. Again, the Constitution extends presidential authority during wartime. Therefore, though technically considered unlawful, Ronal Reagan acted in a scrupulous manner, rendering the right decision, protecting American lives by whatever means necessary. So, in this regard, his actions not only prove consistent with the Constitution, but reflect a reasonable and respectable decision.

Furthermore, serving more than two terms also predisposes limitations, as plausibly evidenced from many presidential incumbents including Wilson, FDR, Nixon, Johnson, Clinton, and George W. Bush. Reagan proved no exception, as his popularity temporarily plummeted to record lows. Again, 8 years lasts a long time when serving as Chief Executive. The probability for blunder proves extremely likely if not inevitable. Nevertheless, Reagan not only survived this debauched scandal, after experiencing public humiliation, but thrived shortly thereafter. "The striking improvement in Soviet-American relations," vanquished all notoriety and ultimately, "salvaged Reagan's presidency," (*American National Biography Online*, 13).

Moreover, and most important, many modern historians neglect a crucial specific fact of circumstance when analyzing Ronald Reagan in regard to Iran-Contra. They often instinctively assign culpability to President Reagan without evaluating the evidence in its entirety. Indeed, one must consider potential exculpatory factors. For example, consider the legal application of mitigating factors to reduce liability. Perhaps the most necessary mitigating factor to truly exonerate Reagan of total blameworthiness in Iran-Contra involves his illness. During the occurrence of Iran-Contra, Reagan underwent hospitalization for colon cancer surgery.

For example, on July 18, 1985, as the scandal occurred, "from his hospital bed," Reagan approved National Security Advisor William McFarlane's aspiration to negotiate with Iran, because he wanted the hostages held in Beirut released (PBS, The American Experience Timeline, 4). Peggy Noonan corroborates this fact. She documents Reagan's convalescence at Bethesda Naval Hospital, which occurred in July 1985, "from surgery for colon cancer" (Noonan, 265). Illness represents an indispensable mitigating factor. Hence, *assuming arguendo* Reagan even accepted the unlawful documents, his diminished capacity resulting from illness, and perhaps mind-altering medication, further impairing sensible judgment, rendered him mentally incompetent to authorize them. Illness compromises capacity. The law requires sufficient capacity to approve any political action. Inadequate capacity ineluctably vindicates liability. Since Reagan obviously lacked sufficient mental capacity necessary for political sanctioning, as persons of ordinary prudence may reasonably infer given his palpable debilitations, the law guarantees exemption from criminal culpability. Therefore, mental incapacity invalidates Reagan's approval, rendering his authorization legally void, thereby exonerating criminal liability. Ultimately, Reagan remains innocent.

Throughout his presidential career, Reagan remained inexorably resolute in containing Soviet influence. He blatantly denounced them as "the focus of evil," (*DeGregorio – The Complete Book of U.S. Presidents, 657*). His anti-Communist temperament never tapered. Reagan intrepidly confronted the USSR. After the Soviet Union, intercepted, "a South Korean Airliner inside Soviet air space, killing 269 people, including

Democratic Representative Lawrence Mc Donald," America, in an attempt to counterattack their voluminous accumulation of medium range missiles aimed at Western Europe, "deployed Pershing and Cruise missiles over Europe on December 1983," (*DeGregorio – The Complete Book of U.S. Presidents, 657*). Again, Reagan preserved his preemptive position with unabated persistence.

Infuriated, Reagan reminded America that only one enemy exists: "The Soviet Union" (*Morris – Dutch, A Memoir of Ronald Reagan*, 553). Cognizant of their rapacious obsession for power, Reagan pondered how the Soviets, "might react to a significant increase in defense spending," He tested his hypothesis, feeling confident that, "the substandard Soviet economy lacked adequate resources to keep pace with the U.S. in an arms race," (PBS - *American Experience – The Presidents, Ronald Reagan*). Apparently, this "rigid Soviet system," proved insufficiently capable of, "responding effectively to the rigorous challenge," presented by Ronald Reagan (Sloan, John, 23). Destined to over-spend them in defense armaments, Reagan's experiment triumphed. Lacking in facilities, the Soviet regime relinquished.

The Reagan administration proposed their national security mechanism, Strategic Defense Initiative (SDI), a space-based missile shield envisioned to encompass Earth. Announced on March 23, 1983, Reagan introduced the technologically sophisticated SDI program, designed to intercept massive missile attacks, required extended surveillance system capabilities, including, advanced weapons possessing "very large electrical power levels and space nuclear reactors," (FAS, 1). Many mainstream liberals considered Reagan a reactionary warmonger. Contrary to popular belief, Reagan frankly despised nuclear weapons. In his national speech summoning "the scientific community" Reagan pronounced,

> "...those who gave us nuclear weapons, to turn their great talents now to the cause of mankind and world peace, to give us the means of rendering these nuclear

> weapons impotent and obsolete," (PBS – The American Experience Timeline, 4).

Although initially "designed to devastate a Soviet offensive strike," the program progressively transitioned toward diminutive systems that sought destruction of, "limited or accidental launches," (Star Wars – Strategic Defense Initiative, 1). While critics condemned the proposal as a "fanciful" Star Wars "fantasy" that violated ABM treaties, it still managed to suppress Soviet resistance (*D'Souza*, 177). Various critics simply condemned it unattainable, identifying Reagan's objective as, "centrally and fundamentally," invalid because supposedly, "it cannot be achieved," (Bundy, Kennan, McNamara, Smith, 166). Yet, history proves these unsubstantiated claims erroneous. By 1987, the U.S. possessed sufficient capability to dismantle, "a major attack," perpetrated by Soviet Strategic Rocket Forces (DefenseLink, 1). A voluminous accumulation, "of American defense spending, continuing previous trends, combined with implicit spending from the SDI, destabilized Soviet resources, transcending their economic limit," (*Gould – The Modern American Presidency, 199*).

Consequently, U.S. proliferation of nuclear weapons superseded Soviet expenditures, instigating their self-destruction, which eventually rendered them unsustainable. The initiative not only proved successful but became a distinguished accomplishment of his presidency. Yet, this tremendous victory remained virtually impossible without the surprising cooperation of Soviet leader Mikhail Gorbachev himself. Obviously, such an achievement also proved insurmountable without the, "exhibited adroitness, flexibility, and prudence that Reagan employed in positive response to Gorbachev's reforms, which included persistent requests for arms cuts and international cooperation," (*American National Biography Online*, 13). The Cold War began to dissipate in 1985, "with the emergence of Mikhail Gorbachev," (*DeGregorio – The Complete Book of U.S. Presidents, 657*).

With Soviet poverty rampant, Gorbachev wanted nothing more than to accommodate the United States (*DeGregorio – The Complete Book of U.S. Presidents, 657*). In actuality, Gorbachev rather, "than lose the arms race and Cold War altogether, he terminated it" (*American National Biography Online*, 11). Moreover, it happened at the most favorable time, following Iran-Contra, "when Reagan desperately needed a stimulus to spark recovery," (*American National Biography Online*, 11).

In fact, "two heartwarming summits with Gorbachev, not only prompted resolution, but allowed Reagan to retire at near pinnacle popularity," (*Nelson –The Presidency and The Political System*, 301). While both summit meetings, "produced little agreement" each initiated advancement in American Soviet relations, (*DeGregorio – The Complete Book of U.S. Presidents, 658*). Hence, Reagan's, "summit meetings with Gorbachev yielded the first treaties in history to reduce nuclear arsenals possessed by both nations," (PBS - *American Experience – The Presidents, Ronald Reagan*).

Reagan first encountered Gorbachev on Tuesday November 19, 1985, at the Geneva summit to construct an arms control agreement. Prior to meeting, Reagan perceived Gorbachev as primarily, "a propagandist determined to alienate America's European allies," (*Morris – Dutch, A Memoir of Ronald Reagan*, 544). After all, with Communism dangerously prevalent, the United States remained in no position to remain passive, or therefore assume any risk of potential threats, most especially after witnessing past attacks. Gorbachev experienced reciprocal apprehension about the United States. Even after the second summit at Iceland in October 1986, Gorbachev still ardently opposed this defensive/offensive shield.

However, after initial confrontation, the pre-existing fear and hostility pervading their preconceived perceptions suddenly subsided. Contrary to initial expectations, Gorbachev appeared "timid" as he approached Reagan (*Morris – Dutch, A Memoir of Ronald Reagan*, 556). Then a sigh of relief overcame his senses, accompanied by a smile, for which he felt, "both simultaneously welcome and caressed," (*Morris – Dutch, A Memoir of Ronald Reagan*, 556). Henceforth, receptivity followed. Reagan's penetrating personality proved the catalyst. His genuinely gregarious demeanor suppressed preceding apprehensions, which triggered an unusual spark of hope between them.

Reagan effectively removed any possibility of suspicion for Gorbachev, leaving the Soviet leader utterly stunned. The first rather mystical impression left both men dumbfounded in incredulous disbelief. Both men seemingly never felt more at ease. As Edmond Morris vividly described, "Gorbachev looked into Reagan's eyes and saw – what? …Only visible in appearance remained the presidential pompadour, glossy and impenetrable. The roaring sky drowned out their initial exchange…Reagan pointed twice, with easy authority, at the steps, inch by inch those two silhouettes, ill-matched in shape and size, yet already companionable, together, moved across memorably, and ascended out of frame," (*Morris – Dutch, A Memoir of Ronald Reagan*, 556). This unique scene as depicted by Morris concluded like a mysterious melodrama of sensationalistic proportions. Yet, the sheer nature of this strange historical phenomenon, barely exaggerates truth.

From that moment forward, reconciliation remained inevitable. The two men established immediate reciprocity. They exchanged conversation. Minutes progressed into hours, listening to each other, debating the issues. Composure continued to sustain, even throughout the plenary session, "where euphoria of intimacy often withers as leaders discuss bilateral business," (*Morris – Dutch, A Memoir of Ronald Reagan*, 560). Gorbachev gracefully stated, "We are not at War with each other, and let's pray God we will never be," (*Morris – Dutch, A Memoir of Ronald Reagan*, 561). The nonchalant invocation of God in addressing peace, sounded awfully strange, spoken from a Marxist-Leninist, most especially, "without deliberation," (*Morris – Dutch, A Memoir of Ronald Reagan*, 561).

Nevertheless, it resonated positively with Reagan. Afterwards, the gentlemen departed in mutual agreement. In a personal interview years later with Morris, Gorbachev himself revealed that when he looked into Reagan's eyes he saw, "Sunshine and clear sky" and while each understood nothing that the other said, Gorbachev instantly sensed a special "authenticity" emanating from his presence; someone possessing immense strength of character or "*Kalibr*" (*Morris – Dutch, A Memoir of Ronald Reagan*, 556).

After firing Donald Regan, including, *inter alia*, numerous other "hard-line advisors connected to Iran Contra in December 1987," Reagan and Gorbachev finally sanctioned a monumental intermediate-range missile reduction (*American National Biography Online,* 13). Nevertheless, as a promising future of interdependence replaced previous Cold War apprehensions, Reagan retired among the most popular presidents in post-World War II America, finishing with an approximate "70% approval rating," (*American National Biography Online*, 13).

Perhaps the most underestimated, grotesquely devalued, aspect of Reagan's diplomatic interactions involves Pope John Paul II and his consummate commitment to conquering communism. As Steve Forbes succinctly stated in an interview, "Pope John Paul was one of the Giants of our era…[he] will be most remembered for his key role in destroying Soviet Communism," (Forbes, Steve, 1 "Great Man Gone—His Legacy Endures). Witnessing its contradictions through internal struggle, John Paul prophesized that, "…Divine providence caused the fall of communism," (Bernstein and Politi, 482).

Indeed, the Pope represented an active proponent of American policy, possessing access to, "carefully guarded secrets, sophisticated political analysis: information from satellites…electronic eavesdropping," etc. (Bernstein and Politi, 482). In his personal memoir Reagan annotated a scheduled conference with, "the Pope's Vatican study team on Nuclear War," which again alludes to Pope John Paul's active political involvement (Brinkley, Reagan, 55). By participating in a Nuclear War study team, Pope John Paul references his active collaboration with confidential U.S. government intelligence to monitor Soviet activities. During his presidential tenure, Ronald Reagan and John Paul II, "worked closely," endorsing the Solidarity labor movement in Poland to suppress Soviet stronghold, exercising dominion throughout Europe (NewsMax Wires, 1).

Ronald Reagan and Pope John Paul II consolidated a collaborative alliance to curtail, contain, and conquer its virulent dissemination. The Pope, a truly devout pacifistic man of unassailable religious faith and benevolence, considered communism dangerous not only to Christianity alone, but humanity itself. The atheistic influence of Soviet Communism, which sought global domination, represented a ruthless disease against religion. Before Gorbachev, Pope John Paul witnessed the malevolent manifestation of Soviet communism first hand through Stalin, who annihilated countless lives to preserve his political power.

By indoctrinating the people with a cancerous mix of unadulterated evil, imposing greed, power, hatred, oppression, death, even torture upon innocent lives, targeting humanity through violence, Pope John Paul recognized a moral duty to actively confront communism, prevent its sacrilegious spread, and ultimately, obliterate it from society. Hence, Pope John Paul, perceived this Godless doctrine which sought destruction to achieve power, as an imminent threat directed against the indispensable faith and existence of humanity. During 1987 at a Meeting with Charities organized in San Antonio, T.X., the Pope, with his sage, saintly words referencing superior intellect and wisdom, verbatim articulated,

> "Social injustice and unjust social structures exist only because individuals and group of individuals deliberately maintain or tolerate them. It is these personal choices, operating through structures, that breed and propagate situations of poverty, oppression, and misery. For this reason, overcoming "social" sin and reforming the social order itself must begin with the conversion of our hearts" (Pope John Paul II, 89-90, "In My Own Words").

Therefore, the Pope, tired of tolerating this oppressive climate created by communism, assumed a bold initiative with Ronald Reagan to trigger its termination. Consider the following commentary offered by William P. Clark, one of President Reagan's most trusted advisers in a 1999 interview. Clark succinctly summarized Reagan's relationship with the Pope, as two courageous crusaders of providence struggled to restore international prosperity through interdependence. According to Clark, Ronald Reagan and Pope John Paul II established a direct collaborative compromise that targeted Soviet Communism, seeking its obliteration. During Reagan's inauguration as President in 1981, Poland became subsumed by Soviet dominion, subjugated to its destructive influence. Clark comments,

> "During his first visit to Poland in 1979, John Paul II encouraged 5 million Poles' [transition] toward moral, spiritual, and political freedom..." Hence, "a natural convergence of interests," facilitated collaboration with the Vatican (Catholic World Report, 1).

By Jan. 20, 1981, when Reagan assumed office, the White house already arranged strategic contacts for alignment against communism (Bernstein, Politi, 257). However, contact officially commenced between Reagan and the Pope in Feb. 1981. Thereafter, both men maintained a close correspondence to plot their annihilation of the global communist threat. In December 1981, the Communist government of Poland exercised its capricious totalitarian reign, arresting countless Polish workers. Months earlier, campaigning for the Republican presidential nomination, Reagan witnessed Poland, "dissolve in rapture," as "tears" swelled his eyes (Bernstein, Politi, 8). Expressing his aggressive posture, Reagan informed the Pope, "the U.S. will not let the Soviet Union dictate Poland's future with impunity," (Riebling, 1). On Dec. 29, 1981, Reagan verbatim composed in a letter addressed to Pope John Paul,

> "I am announcing today additional American measures aimed at raising the cost to the Russians of their continued violence against Poland. ... Unfortunately, if these American measures are not accompanied by

> other Western countries, the Russians may decide to pursue repression, hoping to provoke a rupture within the Western world, while escaping the consequences of our measures. … I therefore ask your assistance in using your own suasion throughout the West in an attempt to achieve unity on these needed measures [economic sanctions on Poland and the Soviet Union]… I hope you will do whatever is in your power to stress these truths to the leaders of the West," (Riebling, 1).

Consequently, acknowledging support for U.S. sanction, the Pope responds in a letter dated Jan. 6, 1982,

> "The Vatican recognizes that the U.S. is a great power with global responsibilities. The United States must operate on the political plane and the Holy See does not comment on the political positions taken by governments. It is for each government to decide its political policies. The Holy See for its part operates on the moral plane. The two planes (politics and morality) can be complementary when they have the same objective. In this case they are complementary because both the Holy See and the United States have the same objective: the restoration of liberty to Poland," (Riebling, 1).

On June 7, 1982, Ronald Reagan and Pope John Paul II met for their first time in person, discussing their concerns for roughly "50 minutes" (*Bernstein*, "The holy alliance", 28). During this, "extraordinary period of U.S.-Vatican collaboration," Ronald Reagan and Pope John Paul II embarked upon a "historic relationship," to conclude communism in Europe (Bernstein, Politi, 270, 280). On June 6, 2004, the day following Ronald Reagan's death, Pope John Paul II paid tribute to him, recollecting, "his efforts to bring down communism that, 'changed the lives of millions of people,' as one Vatican spokesman announced (NewsMax Wires, 1). Therefore, the collaborative compromise between Reagan and Pope John Paul II, who collectively conquered communism, holds monumental significance. Together, they established a diplomatic alliance that deliberately signaled its end. Hence, Pope John Paul and his unprecedented contributions proved necessary to the inevitable defeat of Soviet Communism. Thanks to the Pope and Ronald Reagan, communism saw its destruction.

Reagan also found other constructive methods for conquering communism. For instance, Reagan exercised diplomacy with cooperative nations. In extending U.S. support, he established connections with, "Angola, Afghanistan, and most especially, Central America," to dissuade communist control, (PBS - *American Experience – The Presidents, Ronald Reagan*). Reagan, resurrected the Truman Doctrine, a provision designed to contain communism and hinder its diffusion, empowering anti-Communist regimes located in Africa and Central America.

The Truman Doctrine, instituted by President Harry Truman, promised to provide any nation who summoned U.S. attention, evidencing threat by communist guerilla influence, all necessary military resources, money, arms, and ammunition, for defeating them. Hence, Reagan, like Truman, guaranteed diplomatic alliance, accommodating any nation threatened by Communism. Again, Reagan references his diplomatic dexterity, epitomizing Roosevelt's Corollary, the aphorism, "Speak softly, but carry a big stick." Subsequently known as the Reagan Doctrine, President Reagan expanded the Truman Doctrine to include any nation that feels reasonably threatened by communist influence. On May 5, 1985, Ronald Reagan introduced the Reagan Doctrine, endorsing armed, "insurgencies against Soviet-supported governments," (PBS – The American Experience Timeline, 4). The Reagan Doctrine proved a significant presidential innovation. Unlike the Truman Doctrine, which only sought to thwart communist spread, Reagan advanced one step further. Rather, Reagan initiated a preemptive foreign policy stratagem that surpassed all preceding documents in its scope of intervention. It assumed an aggressive approach to truly contain and conquer communism.

The Reagan Doctrine actually sought, "to reverse Soviet gains," (D'Souza, 152). It aspired in its objective to, "extend and defend freedom," against communism, for other nations seeking political refuge, while simultaneously preventing, "nuclear confrontation," (Nixon, 122). Again, Reagan referenced his superior diplomatic initiative through the Reagan Doctrine, offering an affirmative approach to combat communism, without assuming any bellicose posture. Reagan harnessed his SDI capabilities in conjunction with the Reagan Doctrine to ultimately eradicate communism as an international threat, concluding Cold War atrocities.

As mentioned earlier, Ronald Reagan derived enlightened understanding of foreign policy initiative, acquiring wisdom and knowledge from Larry Beilenson, who influenced his effective foreign policy strategy to a substantial extent. For example, years before initiation of the Reagan Doctrine, Beilenson outlined his fundamental measures in an analysis he entitled "Power through Subversion", which prescribed that American administer sustained assistance for, "dissidents against all communist governments," (Evans, 211). Beilenson recommended "a doctrine" designed to "deal with Communist engendered 'wars'," incorporating maximum range of "political military and economic," resources required for implementation (Evans 211). Evidently, Reagan extracted these sage suggestions and exploited them to his advantage in combating communism.

Unquestionably, Beilenson influenced Reagan. The Reagan Doctrine closely resembled his strategic perspective. Yet, Reagan adapted the basic objectives underlined by Beilenson to suit his own innovative administrative style, in an evolving historical context. Reagan accentuated, "the Jeffersonian universality of freedom," facilitating a democratic framework or, "crusade for freedom," (Lagon, 112). In a poignant "Address to the British Parliament", Reagan's effervescent message which demonstrates undeterred dedication to democracy, embodies the Reagan Doctrine and its principal foreign policy objectives. Through the Reagan Doctrine, Reagan envisioned a "democratic revolution" defined by universal freedom. In the following excerpt, Reagan emphatically elucidates his consummate commitment to conquering communism, and restoring universal freedom:

> "While we must be cautious about forcing the pace of change, we must not hesitate to declare our ultimate objectives and to take concrete actions to move toward them. We must be staunch in our conviction that freedom is not the sole prerogative of a lucky few, but the inalienable and universal right of all human beings," (Ronald Reagan Library, Address to Members of the British Parliament).

Therefore, Reagan's initiation of the Reagan Doctrine proves another conspicuous achievement of his remarkable foreign policy record. Communicating his utopian vision, a leader delivers the legacy of mankind. For Ronald W. Reagan, freedom applies to everyone, transcending gender, race, religion, nationality, etc. The world deserves freedom from oppression. Few modern leaders understood the value of freedom better than Ronald Reagan. His words resurrect the enlightenment philosophy championed by our constitutional founders. Freedom represents the beacon of inspiration, an impetus that provides common salvation to mankind. Restoration of freedom began when Reagan proposed the Reagan Doctrine. It inevitably foreshadowed the end of communism as an international threat to humanity.

Additionally, Reagan even extended so far in application to accommodate military assistance for "friendly governments within the region and supported secret warfare that posed minimal danger toward American lives," (*American National Biography Online*, 11). Reagan offered amnesty to nations who sought cooperation with the U.S., furnishing infrastructural facilities, yet concurrently, exercised authoritative force, only when necessary, targeting and dismantling any power posing a potential threat against American interest. For instance, Reagan authorized nearly $5 billion in fiscal expenditures to buttress the government of tiny El Salvador, "a nominal democracy dominated by reactionary militarists battling left-wing radicalism since 1979," Within days of assuming office, Reagan assisted contra rebels in their, "fight to overthrow the newly installed Marxist led Sandinista regime," (*American National Biography Online*, 11).

Nonetheless, Reagan avoided, "direct military intervention" with other nations, after the lingering aftermath of Vietnam, to secure public interests. As a result of Reagan's relentless persistence against communism, the Soviet Union decomposed and eventually terminated in 1991. On January 11, 1989, Reagan delivered his final address declaring retirement, from the Oval Office, nine days before presidential incumbent George H.W. Bush assumed office (*American National Biography, 13*). Reagan received honorary knighthood, "Knight Grand Cross of the Order of the Bath," in commemoration of his unprecedented contribution to America and the world.

Reagan announced his unfortunate discovery of Alzheimer's disease. However, despite the terminal illness, Reagan still accomplished major achievements post presidential retirement. Reagan published several prominent publications, including anthologies of his speeches and an autobiography which he entitled "An American Life" (Spark Notes, 1). Ronald and Nancy collaborated to establish the Ronald Reagan Foundation, a resourceful educational facility commemorating his unsurpassed historical legacy. On June 5, 2004, Reagan died at the ripe age of 93 in his own home, after battling persistent deteriorating health. "9,277" visited the funeral to pay their respect, including Mikhail Gorbachev and Pope John Paul II (CNN, Americans Line Up to Pay Respect, 1). Ronald Reagan restored moral integrity to American society invigorating patriotism, national faith, and a profound respect for the freedom our constitutional framers so cherished. The Cold War terminated serving as a testament to his unprecedented contributions. He facilitated global peace and bestowed a beacon of inspiration for future democratic initiative in our world. Despite death, the true legacy of a leader lives on forever hereafter.

Conclusion:

Ronald Wilson Reagan, the oldest man and only professional actor ever inaugurated, entered at a time of social discord. A tempestuous period necessitating reform, Reagan provided reconstruction. History inevitably produced the most auspicious conditions for his emergence as an impeccable leader. Reagan's inauguration restored Republican balance to Congress, conservatism in contemporary America. His election resulted in a landslide victory. Determined to provide political reform, his relentless persistence as president progressively ameliorated societal conditions. Reagan championed an aggressive posture in both foreign and domestic relations. Nevertheless, notwithstanding his aggressive stance, he never neglected diplomacy nor diverted from democratic initiative. His foreign policy initiative embodied the Roosevelt Corollary. Following the pithy principle, "Gentle when stroked, fierce when provoked," he maintained isolationism, yet exercised authority against dangerous regimes, while offering peace to amiable nations, particularly those who supported American interests.

By resurrecting the Truman Doctrine, while incorporating diplomatic dexterity with influential leaders, including Soviet leader Mikhail Gorbachev, Reagan contained and curtailed communism, eventually conquering its virulent dissemination. Under the Reagan Doctrine, an expanded version of Truman's Doctrine, he secured peaceful conclusion to

Cold War tensions. In domestic affairs, Reagan sought limited government. He championed federalism, as advocated by our constitutional founders, and reinvented it as a contemporary concept. After witnessing economic deterioration, his implementation of supply side economics and tax reform gradually reversed conditions. Ronald Reagan represented the moral righteousness and dignity of America. In defending justice, he once eloquently proclaimed that, "Life begins when one begins to serve".

Reagan utilized his formidable Christian foundation and virtuous principles to regenerate faith among citizens, restoring the national consciousness of religion, amalgamating America as a principled society. Hence, he not only restored moral providence, but rejuvenated a sense of American patriotism and nationalistic fervor among Americans. Certainly, Ronald Reagan served the U.S. presidency in such a manner that other leaders only aspire to fulfill. Thus, his consummate commitment to America democracy remains unparalleled. Reagan revolutionized the modern American presidency. His profound influence on society, providing conservative reconstruction, conquering communism, revitalizing national prosperity, faith, and moral righteousness while simultaneously renovating America's infrastructure, represents the quintessential paragon for subsequent leaders.

Bibliography

(All Sources Listed in Sequence of Appearance)

Books:

1. DeGregorio, William. A. A Barnes & Noble Book. *"The Complete Book of U.S. Presidents"* 1984, 1989, 1993, 2001, 2002,

2. Gould, Lewis L., "The Modern American Presidency", University Press of Kansas, Library of Congress, 2003

3. Skowronek, Stephen, "The Politics Presidents Make: Leadership from John Adams to Bill Clinton", The President and Fellows of Harvard College, Library of Congress, 1993, 1997

4. D'Souza, Dinesh, "How an Ordinary Man Became an Extraordinary Leader", Touchstone, U.S., Library of Congress, 1999

5. Noonan, Peggy, "When Character Was King", Penguin Books Ltd, U.S., England, 2001

6. Nelson, Michael, "The Presidency and the Political System", Congressional Quarterly, Inc., Library of Congress, 2006

7. Smith, Hendrick, "Reagan, The Man, the President", Macmillan, NY, 1980

8. Evans, Thomas W., "The Education of Ronald Reagan – The General Electric Years and the Untold Story of His Conversion to Conservatism", Columbia University Press, The Mentor Center, L.C., Library of Congress, 2006

9. Sloan, Joan W., "The Reagan Effect—Economics and Presidential Leadership", University Press of Kansas, Library of Congress, 1999

10. Friedman, Thomas, L., "The World is Flat", Douglas & McIntyre Ltd., Canada, U.S., Library of Congress, 2005

11. Reagan, Ronald W., "An American Life", Schuster and Simon, Inc., Library of Congress, 1990

12. Schmalleger, Frank, "Criminal Justice Today – An Introductory Text for the 21st Century", Prentice Hall, Pearsom Custom Publishing, 2007

13. Kernell, Samuel, "Going Public: New Strategies of Presidential Leadership", Washington, D.C., Congressional Quarterly Press, Inc., 1986

14. Edwards III, George, Gallup, Alec M., "Presidential Approval: A Sourcebook", Baltimore, Maryland, Johns Hopkins University Press, 1990

15. Hannity, Sean, "Let Freedom Ring—Winning the War of Liberty Over Liberalism", HarperCollins Publishers, Inc., Library of Congress, 2002

16. Brinkley, Douglas, Reagan Ronald W., "The Reagan Diaries", HarperCollins Publishers, Inc., The Ronald Reagan Presidential Library Foundation, 2007

17. McDonald, Forrest, "The American Presidency: An Intellectual History", University of Press Kansas, Library of Congress, 1994

18. Dye, Thomas, R., "American Federalism – Competition Among Governments", Lexington Books, Library of Congress, 1990

19. Bowman, Ann O., Kearney, Richard C., "State and Local Government, Seventh Edition", Houghton Mifflin Company, Library of Congress, 2008

20. Palmer, John L., Sawhill, Isabel V., "The Reagan Record", Washington D.C., Urban Institute, 1984

21. Conlan, Timothy, "New Federalism – Intergovernmental Reform from Nixon to Reagan", The Brookings Institution, Library of Congress, 1988.

22. Conlan, Timothy, "Federalism and Competing Values in the Reagan Administration", Publius, Winter 1986

23. Edwards, Chris, "Federalism and Separation of Powers – Federal Aid to the States", Federalist Society Journal, Library of Congress, Oct., 2007

24. Coulter, Ann, "How to Talk to a Liberal (If You Must)", Crown Publishing Forum, NY, Library of Congress, 2004

25. Smith, Charles D., "Palestine and the Arab-Israeli Conflict, Sixth Edition", Bedford/St. Martin's, University of Arizona, Library of Congress, 2007

26. Spiegel, Steven, "Other Arab-Israeli Conflict: Making America's Middle East Policy from Truman to Reagan", University of Chicago Press, 1985

27. Schultz, George, Schlesinger, James, McNamara, Robert, Tower, John, Nixon, Richard, Kennan, George, Bundy, Mc George, "The Reagan Foreign Policy", Meridian Book, New American Library, Library of Congress, Council of Foreign Relations. 1981, 1982, 1984, 1985, 1986, 1987,

Article Excerpt Extracts from the book:

Mandelbaum, Michael, "The Luck of the President", p. 133
Schlesinger, James, "Reykavik and Revelations", p. 252-3
Nixon, Richard, "Superpower Summitry", p. 122
Bundy, Kennan, McNamara, Smith, "Star Wars or Arms Control", p. 166

28. Morris, Edmund, "Dutch – A Memoir of Ronald Reagan", Random House, Inc., Simon and Schuster, Library of Congress, 1999

29. Neustadt, Richard E., "Presidential Power and the Modern Presidents: The Politics of Leadership from Roosevelt to Reagan", Macmillan Publishing Company, John Wiley & Sons, Inc., The Free Press, Division of Simon & Schuster, Inc., 1990, 1980, 1960

30. Shaw, Malcolm, "The Modern Presidency", Cambridge University Press, Library of Congress, 2003

31. Ducat, Craig, R., "Constitutional Interpretation – Eighth Edition", Thomson West, Library of Congress, 2004

32. Bernstein, Carl, Politi, Marco, "His Holiness", Doubleday Publishing Group, Inc., Library of Congress, 1996

33. Lagon, Mark P., "The Reagan Doctrine – Sources of American conduct in the Cold War's Last Chapter" Library of Congress, 1994

Articles & Journals:

1. Reagan, Ronald, House UnAmerican Activities Committee Testimony, Oct. 23, 1947, http://www.twcnet.edu/cschutz/history-page/Consensus/Reagan-huac-testimony.html

2. *Time*, "The Powerhouse", January 12, 1959,

3. Encyclopedia, Britannica, Inc., Encyclopedia Britannica Profiles, Early Life and Acting Career, 2007 http://www.britannica.com/presidents/article-214225

4. Schaller, Michael, American National Biography, American Council of Learned Societies, Oxford Press, 2004 www.anb.org/articles/07/07-00791.html

5. The White House, President George W. Bush, "Biography of Ronald Reagan", President Ronald Reagan, Ronald Reagan Library, http://www.whitehouse.gov/history/presidents/rr40.html

6. Linder, Doug, "The Trial of John W. Hinckley Jr.," 2001, http://www.law.umkc.edu/faculty/projects/ftrials/hinckley/hinckleyaccount.html

7. CourtTv, Crime Library, Chapter 8, "This is the Mind", The John Hinckley Case", 2007, Courtroom Television Network, LLC., http://www.crimelibrary.com/terrorists_spies/assassins/john_hinckley/4.html

8. Niskanen, William A., "Reaganomics", The Library of Economics and Liberty, The Concise Encyclopedia of Economics, Liberty Fund, Inc., 1999-2002, http://www.econlib.org/library/Enc/Reaganomics.html

9. Weisbrot, Mark, "Ronald Reagan's Legacy", Common Dreams News Center, Knight-Ridder/Tribune Information Services, June 7, 2004, http://www.commondreams.org/cgi-bin/print.cgi?file=/views04/0607-09.htm

10. Columbia Encyclopedia, Sixth Edition, "Casey, William Joseph," Columbia University Press. 2001-05, http://www.bartleby.com/65/ca/Casey-Wi.html

11. CNN Interactive, Video Almanac, "Reagan Picks First Woman for Supreme Court—July 7, 1981", Cable News Network, Inc., 1998 http://www.cnn.com/resources/video.almanac/1981/index2.html

12. PBS, "The American Experience–Timeline", PBS Online, 1999-2000, http://www.pbs.org/wgbh/amex/reagan/timeline/index_4.html

13. Spartacus Educational, "William Casey", http://www.spartacus.schoolnet.co.uk/JFKcaseyW.htm

14. FAS, Gates, Robert, M., "Iran Contra Report", Chapter 16, http://www.fas.org/irp/offdocs/walsh/chap_16.htm

15. PBS, "American Experience – The Presidents, Ronald Reagan – Foreign Affairs", PBS Online, 2002-2003, http://www.pbs.org/wgbh/amex/presidents/40_reagan/reagan_foreign.html

16. FAS, "Strategic Defense Initiative", http://www.fas.org/nuke/space/c06sdi_1.htm

17. DefenseLINK, "Missile Defense", April 1, 2004, http://www.defenselink.mil/specials/missiledefense/history.html

18. Bernstein, Carl, "The Holy Alliance", *Time*, Feb. 24, 1992, Vol. 139, Issue 8, p28, 8p, 13c, 1bw

19. NewsMax Wires, "Pope: John Paul II: Reagan 'Changed Lives of Millions', June 7, 2004, http://archive.newsmax.com/archives/articles/2004/6/6/130341.shtml

20. Paul II, John, Pope, Chiffolo, Anthony F., "In My Own Words", Library of Congress, 1998

21. Human Events, "Pope John Paul and President Reagan", April 11, 2005,Vol. 61 Issue 13, p10-11, 2p, 4c

22. Riebling, Mark, "Freedom's Men", April 4, 2005, http://www.nationalreview.com/comment/riebling200504040753.asp

23. Spark Notes, "Later Life and Legacy", SparkNotes, LLC, 2006, http://www.sparknotes.com/biography/reagan/section10.rhtml

24. CNN, "Americans Line Up to Pay Respect", June 8, 2004, http://www.cnn.com/2004/ALLPOLITICS/06/07/reagan.main/index.html

Pre-Presidential Speeches:

1. Reagan Library, Reagan, Ronald, "A Time For Choosing", Oct.27, 1964, http://www.reagan.utexas.edu/archives/reference/timechoosing.html

Presidential Speeches:

1. Reagan Library, Reagan, Ronald, "State of the Union Address", Jan. 26, 1982, http://www.reagan.utexas.edu/archives/speeches/1982/12682c.htm

2. Reagan Library, Reagan, Ronald, "Address Before a Joint Session of the Congress on the Program for Economic Recovery," Feb. 18, 1981, http://www.reagan.utexas.edu/archives/speeches/1981/21881a.htm

3. Reagan Library, Reagan, Ronald, "Address to Members of the British Parliament", June 8, 1982, http://www.reagan.utexas.edu/archives/speeches/1982/60882a.htm

4. Reagan Library, Reagan Ronald, "Proclamation 4826 —National Day of Prayer, 1981", March 19, 1981,

Reagan Library Sources:

http://www.reagan.utexas.edu/archives/speeches/1981/31981b.htm
http://www.reagan.utexas.edu/archives/reference/facts.html
http://www.reagan.utexas.edu/archives/speeches/major.html
http://www.reagan.utexas.edu/archives/speeches/1981/81jan.htm
http://www.reagan.utexas.edu/archives/speeches/1981/31981b.htm